Walking Together in Faith

A Workbook for Sponsors of Christian Initiation

THOMAS H. MORRIS

Paulist Press / New York / Mahwah

ISBN: 0-8091-3289-3

Published by Paulist Press
997 Macarthur Boulevard
Mahwah, NJ 07430

Printed and bound in the
United States of America

*Dedicated to my mentors and sponsors over the years,
especially my family, friends, colleagues, and students.*

Contents

Introduction

This handbook started with an invitation to do a workshop with sponsors. While developing the workshop, it occurred to me that most of the resources available were focused on the work of catechists and liturgists in the Order of Christian Initiation of Adults, and that there wasn't very much material around to give to sponsors—either for their formation or for reflection. After working with sponsors, both in the parishes I served with and at workshops around the country, I began to learn of some of the questions and concerns that sponsors were raising with regard to their ministry. Hopefully, this handbook will respond to some of those concerns.

Sponsoring is an important ministry. Sponsors provide the much-needed personal attention and support that catechumens and candidates seek while living through the journey of conversion. For many of us, this understanding of sponsoring is a significant shift from the ceremonial role we have given to sponsors over the years in other sacraments.

My own work with sponsors revealed that the ministry of sponsoring in initiation is very similar to other sponsoring experiences. And so I began to look at those experiences in my life and in other programs and continued to ask: What are the basic skills needed to serve in this way? What I discovered was that sponsoring, in many ways, highlights basic human relational skills, the things we do every day with our families and friends. What was needed was the structuring of those skills in such a way that sponsors could be more focused and intentional in using them. In effect, for most sponsors, it is not a matter of learning new skills. Rather, it is a process of refining and focusing those skills already available to them. Those skills are then supplemented with the particulars of the sponsoring—in this case, an understanding of Christian initiation and the specifics of the Order of Christian Initiation of Adults.

My greatest resources for this handbook were two: the sponsors and communities in my life, and the sponsoring persons themselves whom I have worked with. I am grateful to both sets of people for the rich contributions they have made in my life. Their generosity and care have helped form me into the minister I am today.

My special thanks go to the RCIA community of St. Rose of Lima in Gaithersburg, Maryland.

All text references in this book for the Order of Christian Initiation of Adults come from the 1985 translation entitled *Rite of Christian Initiation of Adults.* Whenever the text is referenced or quoted in this book, a paragraph from the text will be cited, e.g. (n. 9).

Every work such as this handbook involves many people. I am especially grateful to those people who encouraged me to develop this handbook and grappled with me as I struggled to articulate principles and exercises. My work with the North American Forum on the Catechumenate has given me the opportunity to refine some of these thoughts at various workshops. Thanks go to Pat Lynch for the time she took to review parts of the manuscript in its early stages. And special thanks go to those dear friends whose love carried me along in the project—Don Cammiso, Maureen Kelly, Tony Krisak and David Haas. They continue to teach me what is truly valuable and worthy of my time and commitment.

Thomas H. Morris
Third Sunday of Lent 1991

Part One

Christian Initiation

Christian initiation is central to the life of the Christian community. Through the celebration of the rituals of initiation, the Christian community not only births a new church again and again, but is also given an opportunity to recognize and recommit itself to its own identity as a people with a mission: living and proclaiming the reign of God.

The ministry of the sponsor is essential to this birthing and renewing of the church. Sponsors help the catechumens to negotiate and integrate the various levels of interaction that necessarily occur throughout the initiation journey. And sponsors do this as ordinary members of the order of the faithful.

However, the ministry of sponsorship does not happen in isolation. It is immersed in the context of the community of faith and the rich theological foundations that support that community. Part One of this workbook will explore some of those foundations. In particular, sponsors will have the opportunity to reflect on the Order of Christian Initiation of Adults from a variety of perspectives: a general overview of the Order; conversion; the particulars of the sponsoring relationship; and the role of the sponsor in the celebration of initiation.

1

Christian Initiation

Personal Reflection

• *What gives meaning to my life?*

_____

_____

_____

_____

_____

• *What does it mean to be a disciple of Jesus, the Christ?*

_____

_____

_____

_____

_____

• *How does it make a difference to me that I belong to this community of faith?*

_____

_____

_____

_____

• *How am I called to witness to the presence of the reign of God in the world today?*

_____

_____

_____

_____

• *How do we as a parish community welcome new members?*

_____

_____

_____

_____

Christian Initiation

The sacraments of Christian initiation—baptism, confirmation, and eucharist—are celebrations of conversion and discipleship. They ritualize God's call to each of us to follow authentic life-styles that are liberating for all (conversion). They celebrate our committed response that helps make present the awareness of God's abiding and reconciling presence that is available to all (discipleship). Sacraments of initiation, like all other sacraments, are celebrations of the reign of God. They demand that we recognize that we live out of a center deeper and fuller than our very selves: God. Living from that center empowers us for lives of charity, service, justice and compassion.

A stagnant sacramental theology equated sacraments with things we get: we get baptized, we get grace, we get communion. All of the responsibility for sacraments rested outside of the individual and the community. As long as the ritual actions were performed according to the law, and the community was properly disposed, then we could have sacraments. A renewed sense of sacraments shifts from this objective, sterile view of sacraments to one that is dynamic, empowering and relational. Sacraments are about God's active and empowering love with and for us. They are focused moments of celebration that bring to heightened awareness the saving power and love of God for all people in the ordinary of our lives. Furthermore, sacraments are not simply for *us*. That is, we don't celebrate sacraments so we can *get* something for ourselves. Rather, we celebrate sacraments in order to be empowered for more authentic and faithful service of the mission of the reign of God. Sacraments point us outward: service for our sisters and brothers.

Sacraments of Christian initiation provide the focus for understanding the other sacraments of the community. Initiation sacraments celebrate: freedom from sin, an identity as sons and daughters of God, the gift of the Spirit, the configuration into the Christ, and the nourishment of the very presence of the Lord. They celebrate all of these within a context—our call to live as disciples of Jesus, the Christ. Because we have experienced liberation from sin, because we know ourselves as God's children, because we know the abiding presence of the Spirit, because we are configured to be like the Christ, because we are nourished by the very life of God, then we can live as faithful witnesses to the good news of God's presence in the world, made flesh in Jesus, the Christ. This presence of God offers freedom and reconciliation, meaning and hope. In a word—salvation. The sacraments of initiation, therefore, are sacraments of commitment to a life-style. The other sacramental celebrations depend on this sense of sacrament to make any sense. The sacraments of healing—reconciliation and anointing of the sick—recognize that we are not always faithful to this covenant and need to welcome God's healing forgiveness (reconciliation), or that members of the community experience illness that calls for the support of the whole community (anointing of the sick). The sacraments of vocation—matrimony and holy orders—reflect two ways that adults live out their initiation commitments.

The Christian community, therefore, takes the commitment of initiation very seriously. The concern is not just membership, but people making full, active and conscious choices about the shape and quality of their life-styles. That is why when the reformers of Vatican Council II called for the restoration of the catechumenate, they were not simply digging up a practice from the early church, but rather, recognized in this ancient process a timeless model of formation or tutoring in Christian discipleship. This model included a period of apprenticeship with the community, surrounded by the word of God, worship, service, prayer, and the very life of the community. Within this environment, one could begin to grapple honestly with God's invitations to Christian discipleship, a grappling we name "conversion." Thus, the restoration of the adult catechumenate process for Christian initiation highlights those essential components for sacramental initiation. We call this process the Order of Christian Initiation of Adults (the early translation of this collection of rites was rendered Rite of Christian Initiation of Adults, and hence the popular acronym, RCIA).

There are many Catholics who say that we demand too much of adults entering the church today, that they are glad they never had to go through what they are going through, and other similar comments. Perhaps these are Catholics who do not yet understand the implications of making an adult commitment for Christian discipleship. We would never presume that one would make a life commitment with another person in matrimony after a short period of dating. Oh, that's different, some will say. But is it that different? Is the choice to commit oneself to the mission of the reign of God, to be about the life-style of Jesus, the Christ any less an important decision?

Christian initiation is a slow process that helps us—both as individuals and as a community—begin to name the great works of God in life, and how we are gifted for service in the name of God. It is a process of freedom and liberation. But it takes time, support and care. It is the responsibility of the entire parish community to create the environment in which one can grow in this awareness of God's call (*RCIA*, n. 9). When we begin to shift our focus from a quick-fix baptism to a lifetime commitment of discipleship, we begin to relax in the process, and to recognize that all of us are involved in Christian initiation again and again. Each

time we gather at the table of the eucharist, we are called to commit ourselves again to the mission of the reign of God.

Thus, those coming to our community are important symbols to us of our own ongoing initiation commitment. They remind us—especially through the ritual celebrations—of our own stories of faith. Communities of faith relive their own journeys of conversion with these inquirers, catechumens, candidates, elect and neophytes. They remind us of our identity: people of water, oil, and the table who are sent to proclaim the good word: Jesus, our salvation.

• *Regarding my ministry as a sponsor, I learned in this section that:*

_____

_____

_____

• *Issues that I need further clarification on from this section are:*

_____

_____

_____

• *After discussing with your coordinator of sponsors, note some of those clarifications for future reference:*

_____

_____

_____

What Is the Order of Christian Initiation of Adults?

The Order of Christian Initiation of Adults was the last of the sacramental rites revised after Vatican Council II. Promulgated in 1972, it heralded a shift in the practice of celebrating the sacramental initiation of adults in the church. The earlier practice had been convert classes or instruction, usually given by the parish priest to the individual, followed by a private celebration of baptism and eucharist. The restoration of the catechumenate moves us away from concerns of membership (the *right* information) that seemed to dictate the previous practice, to initiation formation that is focused on the process of conversion and one's response within the context of a community of faith. This is not to suggest that people who entered the church before the restored catechumenate were not serious about their experience of conversion. However, the programs we provided them celebrated the cerebral dimensions of faith (doctrinal formulations), often to the neglect of other dimensions of conversion. The Order of Christian Initiation of Adults provides a ritual structure and suggests a formation process wherein a more holistic and integrated response to religious conversion can occur. In effect, the Order does not only change the procedure for welcoming new members into the church, but the very structures upon which one builds such procedures have been radically changed and transformed. This transformation of initiation structures has far-reaching effects beyond the celebration of the RCIA because it calls us to examine our understanding and celebration of baptismal covenant, the other ritual sacrament celebrations, and the mission that guides and directs our identity as church.

A provisional English translation of the Order of Christian Initiation of Adults was issued in 1974. Many thought this text was optional. However, this was not the case. Despite this misunderstanding, several parishes began the implementation of the Order. In 1986, the National Conference of Catholic Bishops (NCCB) issued an official translation of the Order of Christian Initiation of Adults for use in the dioceses of the United States, which also included separate rites for baptized, combined rites and national statutes for implementation. These combined rites were a response to the pastoral experiences of many involved in initiation: a number of adults who were coming to the community had already been baptized, either in another Christian community or in the Catholic community. The combined rites now provide initiation structures for use with both the unbaptized and baptized. This new edition of the Order of Christian Initiation of Adults, published in 1988, called for implementation in all dioceses of the United States, beginning in September, 1988.

The Order of Christian Initiation of Adults is a restoration of the ancient practice of initiation in the church, and is divided into various periods and steps that respect and support the individual's journey in faith. The periods and their accompanying transition celebrations or steps are: the Period of Evangelization or Precatechumenate, the Rite of Acceptance into the Order of Catechumens, the

Order of Christian Initiation of Adults

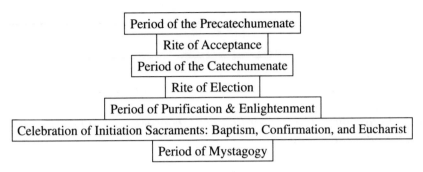

Figure 1

Period of the Catechumenate, the Rite of Election, the Period of Purification and Enlightenment, the Celebration of the Sacraments of Initiation (baptism, confirmation, eucharist), and the Period of Postbaptismal Catechesis or Mystagogy.

The Order of Christian Initiation of Adults is a profoundly intricate weaving of various threads: rich evangelization, authentic hospitality and welcome, catechesis centered on the lectionary (i.e., the Sunday mass scripture readings), witness in the liturgical assembly based on one's conversion story, music that integrates the conversion experiences with the community's worship, presiders familiar with the stories of the catechumens, and a parish community willing to commit themselves to people with whom they have grown in faith. The threads of catechesis, liturgical ministries, parish witness and community, liturgical music, and sponsorship are woven together to create this event we call initiation. Without the particular threads, we risk empty rituals and disconnected catechesis. With these threads, initiation can become an opportunity to help people discern God's call to embrace the cross of Jesus, the Christ in the midst of this particular Christian community.

• *Regarding my ministry as a sponsor, I learned in this section that:*

_____

_____

_____

• Issues that I need further clarification on from this section are:

_____

_____

_____

• After discussing with your coordinator of sponsors, note some of those clarifications for future reference:

_____

_____

_____

Period of Evangelization and Precatechumenate

The period of precatechumenate takes place when the individual begins to respond to a personal desire to seek God within this particular community of Catholic Christians. The reasons vary and are as many as there are individuals. This is a period of searching, asking questions, and the initial stirrings of faith.

During the precatechumenate, stories of the Catholic community are told to the inquirer: gospel stories, stories about the Catholic Church, personal stories of faith, and the stories of the parish. Gathering regularly with members of the community, these inquirers raise the questions and concerns they have about following the Lord in the Catholic community. The goal of this period of formation is to help the inquirers come to an initial awareness of God's saving presence in their lives, and to help them discern their initial readiness to embrace the way of life of Jesus, the Christ. In addition to the support and direction from the precatechumenate team members, sponsors chosen from the community begin a special ministry of accompaniment with the inquirers to help them in discerning their readiness to embrace the gospel way of life more fully. While the inquirers usually meet as a group, the period of the precatechumenate lasts as long as each inquirer needs— this is a period of no fixed duration—thus respecting the individual's journey of faith.

• *Regarding my ministry as a sponsor, I learned in this section that:*

_____

_____

_____

• *Issues that I need further clarification on from this section are:*

_____

_____

_____

• *After discussing with your coordinator of sponsors, note some of those clarifications for future reference:*

_____

_____

_____

First Step: Rite of Acceptance into the Order of Catechumens

The rite of acceptance into the order of catechumens is the first of the public rites celebrated in the Order of Christian Initiation of Adults. During this important ritual, the inquirers publicly declare their intention to continue their journey toward full initiation in the Catholic Church, and the community accepts them, offering its support and witness during the journey. The ritual text is clear about its expectations of those who make this first step: "The prerequisite for making this first step is that the beginnings of the spiritual life and the fundamentals of Christian teaching have taken root in the candidates" (*RCIA*, n. 42).

PRE-RESA-QUIT

The rite, celebrated at various times during the year depending on need, consists of various parts: receiving the candidates, the liturgy of the word, and the dismissal of the candidates. During the receiving of the candidates, the community goes in procession to greet the candidates who are waiting to come to the gathering of the assembly. Ideally, the candidates and their sponsors are assembled outside of the church building itself to mark their passage into the worship and life of the community. During this time, sponsors introduce the candidates and provide initial testimony on behalf of the candidates. The presider then asks the candidates what it is they want from God and from this community. After making clear their intentions, the candidates are then invited to accept the gospel as a way of life. At this key moment in the ritual, the candidates publicly affirm their desire to embrace the gospel life-style. This affirmation provides the context for the remainder of the ritual, as well as the focus for the whole catechumenate process. Following the affirmation, the whole body of each candidate is signed with the cross, the symbol of the new way of life they will follow. Now the candidates are called catechumens, that is, those within whom the word echoes and resounds.

The liturgy of the word is celebrated, and the homily brings together the various threads of the ritual for the catechumens and the community. The rite continues with an optional presentation of the scriptures, prayers of petition, and a prayer over the catechumens.

The rite calls for the dismissal of the catechumens from the assembly before the liturgy of the eucharist (*RCIA,* n. 67), and notes that this dismissal is celebrated each week throughout the catechumenate process (*RCIA,* n. 75.3). The dismissal rite is a positive gesture of hospitality to the catechumens. They are not yet welcomed at the table of the eucharist, so we send them forth together to continue their own formation around the table of the word they have just heard proclaimed. The dismissal rite is not a movement *from* the community, but a movement *to* a continued gathering with members of the community (the catechumenate team and sponsors) that focuses specifically on the issues of Catholic Christian life as they emerge in the "breaking open of the word."

• *Regarding my ministry as a sponsor, I learned in this section that:*

_____

_____

_____

• *Issues that I need further clarification on from this section are:*

_____

_____

_____

• *After discussing with your coordinator of sponsors, note some of those clarifications for future reference:*

_____

_____

_____

Period of the Catechumenate

The period of the catechumenate is a prolonged period of formation in the Christian life. The Order of Christian Initiation of Adults notes that maturity in faith during the period of the catechumenate is achieved in four ways: catechetical, spiritual, liturgical and apostolic formation (*RCIA,* n. 75). The primary catechetical text for the catechumenate is the lectionary (i.e., the book of scripture readings used at mass) from which flows the basic issues of Catholic life and teaching. The catechumens are supported in their life of prayer and growth by their sponsors, the catechumenate team, and the whole of the Christian community. Throughout the catechumenate, the catechumens are nourished and purified by appropriate liturgical celebrations, including the Sunday liturgy of the word with the assembly. And the catechumens, because they experience God's call to be servant for one another, begin to commit themselves to works of justice and charity through lives of apostolic service that flow from their experience of the gospel. The catechumens learn the Christian way of life from the Christian community and the community's participation in its own faith.

Ordinarily, the catechumens gather with their sponsors—who serve as companions—for the Sunday celebration of the liturgy of the word with the parish community. After the homily, they will be "kindly dismissed" (*RCIA,* n. 75.3) to continue feeding on the word of God. During this time together, they will explore the Sunday scripture texts together and raise up from them the issues of Catholic Christian life.

During the period of the catechumenate there are many liturgical celebrations. In addition to the liturgy of the word and dismissal catechesis already noted, the catechumens participate in other rites: celebrations of the word, minor exorcisms, blessings, anointings, presentations of the Creed and the Lord's Prayer (*RCIA,* nos. 81–105). All of these liturgical celebrations strengthen the catechumens in their conversion journey of faith, as well as witness to God's love for them.

The period of the catechumenate is of different duration for each catechumen. "The time spent in the catechumenate should be long enough—several years if necessary—for the conversion and faith of the catechumens to become strong" (*RCIA,* n. 76).

• *Regarding my ministry as a sponsor, I learned in this section that:*

_____

_____

_____

• *The issues that I need further clarification on from this section are:*

_____

_____

_____

• *After discussing with your coordinator of sponsors, note some of those clarifications for future reference:*

_____

_____

_____

Second Step: The Rite of Election

The rite of election brings to an end the period of the catechumenate and inaugurates the period of purification. It is usually celebrated on the First Sunday of Lent. The discernment for election is guided by these principles from the rite: "The catechumens are expected to have undergone a conversion in mind and in action and to have developed a sufficient acquaintance with Christian teaching as well as a spirit of faith and charity" (*RCIA*, n. 120).

The appropriate place for the rite of election is the cathedral church, celebrated by the bishop. The ritual text approved for use in the United States includes a parish rite to send catechumens for election by the bishop (*RCIA*, nos. 108–117).

The rite occurs during the liturgy of the word, following the homily. The catechumens are presented to the community, after which time the godparents, sponsors and other members of the assembly are invited to give testimony about the catechumens' readiness to be admitted to the initiation sacraments. Following this period of testimony, the catechumens are called to the celebration of the Easter sacraments (baptism, confirmation, and eucharist) and are then invited to offer their names for enrollment in the book of the elect. Most of the ritual to this point can take place at the local parish community, after which the catechumens are remembered in prayer and dismissed from the assembly to go to the continuation of the rite at the cathedral. Often the cathedral liturgy will follow the structure outlined above, but with less time for spontaneous witness. Also, if there are many catechumens, the enrollment of names may simply be the presentation of the book of the elect to the bishop (presuming the enrollment has already happened in the parish).

After the enrollment at the cathedral liturgy, the bishop declares the catechumens to be members of the elect, that is, those chosen to celebrate the sacraments of initiation at the Easter Vigil. After a brief instruction to the catechumens and their godparents, there are prayers of intercession, a prayer over the elect, and the dismissal of the elect.

It is at the rite of election that the godparents begin their formal role in the initiation process. However, for godparents to authentically witness to the story of conversion of the elect, they need to be part of the journey with them well before the celebration of the rite of election. The sponsor from the parish community continues as a support to the elect at this time and throughout the remainder of the process.

• *Regarding my ministry as a sponsor, I learned in this section that:*

_____

_____

_____

• *Issues that I need further clarification on from this section are:*

_____

_____

_____

• *After discussing with your coordinator of sponsors, note some of those clarifications for future reference:*

_____

_____

_____

Period of Purification and Enlightenment

The period of purification and enlightenment is a time of intense spiritual preparation that occurs during Lent. The focus of this period is twofold: the final preparation of the elect for the Easter sacraments through prayer and penance, and the challenge to the local community to enter more deeply the cycle of the Paschal Mystery through the witness of the elect and their conversion journey. During this period there are specific rites that help bring about this purification and enlightenment: scrutinies, presentations of the Creed and the Lord's Prayer, and the preparation rites for initiation.

Three scrutinies are celebrated on the Third, Fourth, and Fifth Sundays of Lent. The scrutinies are celebrations of healing and strengthening: helping to uncover and heal all that is sinful as well as raising up and strengthening all that is good in the lives of the elect. The scrutinies are celebrated during the liturgy of the word, following the homily. The scriptures come from the Cycle A readings of the lectionary (*RCIA,* n. 146) because they help expose our growing need for God: the woman at the well, the man born blind, and the raising of Lazarus. The assembly and the elect are called to silent prayer to reflect on their sin and need for God's freedom. This silent prayer is followed by intercessions that address the areas of sin that keep the elect, the community, the church and the world in bondage. After this recognition of sin, the presider continues with the prayer of exorcism. Exorcism prayers are petitionary prayers for freedom. They help us recognize there are areas in each of our lives that are not free from sin. In the exorcisms, we pray that God's Spirit may breathe life into those dead areas, setting all free to respond more fully to the gospel. After these prayers for freedom (exorcism prayers), the elect are dismissed and the community continues with the liturgy of the eucharist.

The presentations of the Creed and the Lord's Prayer occur during the third and fifth weeks of Lent, unless they have been anticipated during the period of the catechumenate. Often the presentations are anticipated because of the relatively short time of the period of enlightenment. Whenever they are celebrated, it is essential that they are celebrated with the local community. The community now presents to the women and men chosen to celebrate the Easter sacraments some of the most treasured gifts of the community's faith and prayer: the Creed and the Lord's Prayer. The Creed is the foundational proclamation of the Christian faith, a summary of the truths experienced by the Christian community. The community recognizes the ability of the elect to now embrace this maturing faith and asks that they commit the Creed to the memory of both head and heart. The elect will later publicly recite this Creed at the preparation rites. The Lord's Prayer is the prayer of those who experience themselves as daughters and sons of God. The community expresses its deep desire to share that life with the elect through the gift of the Lord's Prayer. At the Easter Vigil, the elect will recite the Lord's Prayer with the community for the first time.

• *Regarding my ministry as a sponsor, I learned in this section that:*

_____

_____

_____

• Issues that I need further clarification on from this section are:

_____

_____

_____

• After discussing with your coordinator of sponsors, note some of those clarifica-
tions for future reference:

_____

_____

_____

Third Step: Celebration of the Sacraments of Initiation

The sacraments of initiation—baptism, confirmation, eucharist—are celebrated at the Easter Vigil. As the parish community assembles to celebrate the central mysteries of our faith—the Paschal Mystery—the community also welcomes men and women into the power and life of Christ's death and resurrection. Through the celebration of the Easter sacraments, the elect experience the forgiveness of sin, celebrate their identity as daughters and sons of God, share in the mission of Jesus, and become full members of the Catholic communion.

The celebration of baptism follows the service of light and the liturgy of the word during the vigil. After an appropriate procession to the baptismal bath, the presider invites the community to pray for the candidates who are asking for baptism. After silent prayer, the community sings the litany of the saints, a symbol of the communion of the church that extends beyond all space and time. Following the litany, the baptismal waters are blessed, recalling the great deeds of God and invoking the power and presence of the Trinity. The candidates for baptism are then invited to renounce sin and to profess faith in the Paschal Mystery into which they will be baptized. Immediately following this profession, the elect come forward for the baptismal washing, the water rite—either through immersion or by the pouring of water and the proclamation of the trinitarian formula: I baptize you in the name of the Father, and of the Son, and of the Holy Spirit. The newly baptized are then clothed with the baptismal garment and presented with a candle lit from the Easter candle, both symbols of their new way of life.

The celebration of confirmation follows the baptismal rite. After the invitation to silent prayer for the outpouring of the Spirit, the presider continues with the laying on of hands, the ancient symbol-gesture of invoking the power and presence of the Spirit. The baptismal commitment is then sealed by the anointing with chrism. After the celebration of confirmation, the community renews its baptismal promises and the newly baptized and confirmed are led to their places within the assembly. These new members of the community are now called neophytes, the "newly planted."

During the celebration of the eucharist, the neophytes participate fully for the first time in the prayer of the community. They are welcomed to the table of the eucharist and share in the body and blood of Christ, thus being strengthened for this new way of life they are embracing.

• *Regarding my ministry as a sponsor, I learned in this section that:*

_____

_____

_____

• *Issues that I need further clarification on from this section are:*

_____

_____

_____

• *After discussing with your coordinator of sponsors, note some of those clarifications for future reference:*

_____

_____

_____

Period of Postbaptismal Catechesis or Mystagogy

Sacramental initiation does not end at the Easter sacraments. The Order of Christian Initiation of Adults provides for another period of formation, the period of mystagogy, that is, reflection on the mysteries. The neophytes, along with the community, reflect together on the celebration of the Easter mysteries—the Paschal Mystery—and begin the process of making it a full and active part of their lives. The ritual text specifies how this is accomplished: "through meditation on the Gospel, sharing in the eucharist, and doing works of charity" (*RCIA,* n. 244). The primary center for this ongoing formation is the Sunday assembly. Additionally, the neophytes often continue to gather with their sponsors and the intitiation team to continue to break open the word and explore the meaning of the experience of the sacraments for their lives. The formal period of formation continues through Pentecost, the feast of mission. The guidelines for the implementation of the *RCIA* in the United States also call for ongoing mystagogy for at least one year following sacramental initiation (National Statutes, n. 24).

The Easter season, the season of feasting, is celebrated by the entire community. The neophytes gather at the Sunday assembly with the community, witness to their experiences of God for the community, and participate in the planning and celebration of the eucharist. They are leaven for new life in the community; they are one source of renewal. Together, the neophytes and community discern their gifts and recognize their responsibility to serve the mission of the reign of God. Mystagogy brings to a close the formal initiation process and begins the lifelong challenge of discipleship.

• *Regarding my ministry as a sponsor, I learned in this section that:*

_____

_____

_____

• *Issues that I need further clarification on from this section are:*

_____

_____

• After discussing with your coordinator of sponsors, note some of those clarifications for future reference:

_____

_____

_____

Adaptations for Those Baptized

The description above of the periods and stages of the Order of Christian Initiation of Adults presumes candidates for full sacramental initiation—baptism, confirmation, eucharist—who have not been baptized. However, as noted earlier, the approved edition for use in the United States includes rituals for baptized adults. Who are these adults and how does a parish know when to celebrate the Order with them?

If someone has been baptized—in the Catholic community or in another Christian community—but was not catechized (that is, was not formed in the life of the community through prayer, participation in the life of the community, religious education, community worship, and celebration of the other sacraments of initiation: confirmation and eucharist), then that adult also celebrates the Order with the appropriate adaptations (cf. *RCIA*, Part II, Chapter 4, nos. 400ff.).

If someone has been baptized and catechized in another Christian community, but seeks to celebrate full communion in the Roman Catholic Church, then an abbreviated process modeled on the *RCIA* is used (cf. *RCIA*, Part II, Chapter 5, nos. 473ff.).

If someone, however, has been baptized in the Catholic community, has celebrated eucharist or confirmation, and has had basic catechesis, then that adult is not enrolled in the Order of Christian Initiation of Adults. The parish needs to provide a different formation process that is accommodated to the needs of this adult. Such a process would benefit by including the foundational principles of initiation.

What are the appropriate adaptations for persons who are baptized? The ritual text recognizes that their experience of faith and conversion is often different from someone who is not baptized. Depending upon the community of faith from which they come, some may have very rich experiences of discipleship, and therefore will need a short period of formation. Others will come with very little experience in a religious community, and will require more time to be tutored in the ways of discipleship. Therefore, the rite recommends the same structure for the discernment of the journey of conversion but also recognizes that the time frame will be different. Eventually, parishes will be comfortable providing an ongoing precatechumenate and catechumenate process into which people move freely at different times of the year depending on their needs and growth in faith.

Ritually, the community affirms the baptism of the candidate and wants to help the candidate realize the power of that baptism. Furthermore, rites appropriate only for the unbaptized or uncatechized (such as the presentations of the Creed and the Lord's Prayer) are not celebrated with candidates for full communion who have been previously catechized (cf. *RCIA*, n. 407). There is current discussion regarding the appropriateness of candidates celebrating scrutinies and some of the other rituals. The present rite calls for a ritual similar to the scrutinies —a penitential rite (*RCIA*, n. 459f.)—held on the Second Sunday of Lent. The RCIA team in a parish, keeping abreast of these discussions, will provide the candidates with rituals that remain sensitive to their needs and experience.

Hence, uncatechized candidates are in the RCIA process for an extended period of formation and usually celebrate full initiation at Easter (*RCIA*, n. 409), although full communion with adults who are baptized and catechized is to be celebrated whenever they are ready (*RCIA*, n. 478).

• *Regarding my ministry as a sponsor, I learned in this section that:*

_____

_____

_____

• *Issues that I need further clarification on from this section are:*

_____

_____

_____

• *After discussing with your coordinator of sponsors, note some of those clarifications for future reference:*

_____

_____

_____

Time Line

When does all this happen? If I become involved with the Order of Christian Initiation of Adults, how long will it take? These are usual questions of sponsors, especially if they are new. Unfortunately, there are no easy answers.

The Order of Christian Initiation of Adults attempts to hold in creative tension the individual journey of faith of the catechumen or candidate within the context of the community of faith. Both dimensions are necessary and both dimensions dictate the time line of the Order.

Regarding the catechumen or candidate, we respect the movement of grace that calls one to conversion. That happens at different times for different people. Thus, we cannot set up rigid programs with "set" calendar dates (such as, the precatechumenate begins in mid-September, and the rite of acceptance will be celebrated the First Sunday of Advent). Thus, the precatechumenate needs to be readily available all year long (and flexible enough) to integrate new inquirers. With such flexibility, it will also be necessary to celebrate the rite of acceptance at various times throughout the year.

Regarding the community of faith, we also respect the liturgical calendar that helps establish the rhythm of Christian living. Thus, if someone is ready to celebrate full sacramental initiation in early January, we delay celebration until the community's primary season of initiation: the Easter Vigil and Easter season. Or given the rhythm of the liturgical calendar, it is more appropriate to celebrate the rite of acceptance during Ordinary Time (i.e., ordinal or counted time).

These are some examples of the scheduling differences that affect everyone involved. It is safe to say that if you are sponsoring a catechumen, you will be

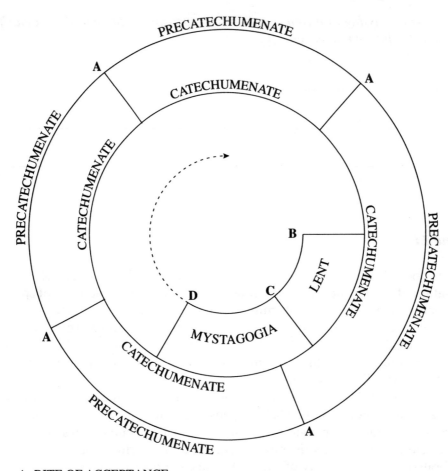

A - RITE OF ACCEPTANCE
B - RITE OF ELECTION
C - EASTER SACRAMENTS
D - PENTECOST

Figure 2

involved with initiation for at least one year until initiation, and then the period of mystagogy that follows. If you are sponsoring someone who is coming into full communion with the Catholic Church from another Christian tradition, the period of preparation will be adjusted to meet his or her needs as well as the community's liturgical life.

The time line for initiation, rather than a straight line with clear dates and deadlines, is cyclic, accommodated to the liturgical year, as illustrated on page 24.

RCIA: Another Program?

These reflections on the Order of Christian Initiation of Adults can lead one to think: one more program! How do we convince the parish to get involved in this program? Such thinking will lead nowhere because initiation is not a program. It is a sacramental rite of the church and therefore reflects the church's understanding of the process of conversion. We will not be able to convince anyone to accept the Order because we cannot convince anyone into conversion. Rather, the Order will need to be celebrated well and, by that very celebrating, it will draw the parish community into an active awareness and participation in the demands of initiation. The Order of Christian Initiation of Adults is not optional—it is the way the Roman Catholic Church celebrates the initiative of God in the lives of people coming to our community, as well as deepening the awareness and commitment of the parish community. If we allow it to stand on its own in the parish community (rather than being one more program we have to do), we will discover a wealth of wisdom and insight in helping both individuals and the community recognize and respond to the compassionate presence of God in our midst, calling us to freedom and salvation.

2

Conversion: Falling in Love

Introduction

Christian conversion is about being in love. It is the process of discovering one's true identity as living with and for others in authentic self-sacrificing love. It is a transformation and restructuring of how individuals and communities face life, causing them to change, to turn around, to live life in more authentic ways. It is the reordering of our lives in such a way that we recognize God as our center and the mission of the reign of God as our life-style and vocation. Christian conversion grounds this in the experience of Jesus, the Christ.

Exercise: Personal Reflection

• *Recall a period in your life, an event, or a relationship in which, in hindsight, you recognize the situation clearly changed and changed you in some way.*
• *Identify the event or relationship:*

_____

_____

• *Describe the event or relationship when you felt it was secure, predictable, perhaps safe:*

_____

_____

_____

_____

_____

• *What began to happen to change this?*

_____

_____

_____

_____

_____

• *How did you feel at this time?*

_____

_____

_____

_____

• List the movements the situation seemed to go through and how you felt during each movement:

• _____

• _____

• _____

• _____

• _____

• _____

• What brought about the final change?

_____

_____

_____

_____

_____

• How are you different because of this?

_____

_____

_____

_____

_____

• Try to identify the change by stating it in a From-To statement; e.g., it was a change from isolation to relationship:

_____

_____

• What did you learn about yourself, others, God?

_____

_____

_____

_____

_____

Conversion

The human person and the human community are created for responsible living. By embracing truly authentic life-styles, the human community has the capacity for transcendence, i.e., going beyond personal wants in order to embrace universal values, the values of the reign of God. Living life grounded in such values brings meaning and direction to life. Rather than choosing to live in the cycle of sin, human beings have the choice to live their true identity as free, loving, and just persons, as daughters and sons of God. When we are unfaithful to such authentic life-styles, we experience alienation from ourselves, from others, and from God. In effect, we choose sin.

The consistent message of the Judeo-Christian communities has been: "Reform your life! Turn from sin!" Concretely, this is a call to allow the power of God's love to restore order to ourselves and our communities. It is a call to transform the impaired values that dictate and manipulate people's life choices into true and authentic values that breathe the power of God's Spirit. Conversion—this process of reform and turning—is both an act of repentance and an act of acceptance. As an act of repentance, it is the turning away from all that refuses to be truly valuable.

As an act of acceptance, it is the recognition that the very ability to make new choices is a pure gift of grace, inviting us to receive and respond with courage and humility. Conversion has more to do with the recognition of our heart's desire to be congruent with God's desires and less to do with our wallowing in self-abasement and pity. That is not to say conversion is easy. In fact, it is quite the opposite. But the painfulness comes from our realization of our infidelity and alienation. In the face of such love, how could we not feel remorse and deep sorrow? The journey of conversion is a journey to wholeness.

Central to Christian living—and therefore at the heart of the initiation process—is conversion. Conversion is the "turning around" of our attitudes, affect, intellect, will—our whole person—to face ourselves, others and the world with the vision of God. Often we view conversion as a once-in-a-lifetime experience, similar to the story of St. Paul on the road to Damascus. While such radical experiences of conversion do happen, they are usually the culmination of a series of events. Also, this conversion moment also serves as a turning point. The process or journey of conversion, however, is not completed in that "moment."

Authentic conversion results in the transformation of consciousness that elicits a whole new quality of being—we don't see new things; we see things in new ways. We embrace the values of the reign of God as normative. While there is a continuing and deepening process of internalizing these values throughout one's life, they are rooted in this fundamental and radical shift of consciousness, the authenticity of which is manifested by the fruits of one's life-style.

It is important to remember that: (1) Conversion is primarily the action of God. When we speak about conversion, we are talking about the radical in-breaking of God's love into human life and activity, embracing us with compassion and mercy. It is fundamentally God's desire to embrace us into the fullness of life with God's love and life. (2) Conversion is about our openness to accept the mercy and freedom of God. God respects human freedom and would never force a relationship with us. Yet God continues to beckon, call, allure, invite, entice us into God's loving embrace. Perhaps on levels deeper than our conscious awareness, we make explicit choices to welcome the initiative of God. For various reasons—usually fear—we often barricade our hearts and do not allow this relationship to touch and transform us. (3) This encounter with grace demands a new life-style—gospel life-style. That is why the experience of conversion is multilayered, affecting every dimension of life. Our instinctive reaction to people who thump their Bibles and use religious language but do not embody those values consistently gives evidence to us of our basic sense that conversion is full-personed. "Praise the Lord" without a life-style patterned on true gospel values is akin to a "noisy gong or a clanging bell."

Many theologians, most particularly Bernard Lonergan, have written on conversion. The fruit of their reflection is that, fundamentally, conversion is falling in love with God in an unrestricted manner. That does not mean that because we are focused on God, everything else is unimportant. It is quite the opposite. All of life is recognized as holy because of God. It is not "God" *or* the "other," but God *through* the other, God awakening us *to* the other. Falling in love with God expands the heart to true and authentic agape. That deepens and enhances our loves, our work, our life together for the transformation of the world. St. Augustine captures this when he claims: "Love God and do as you will." If we truly love God, all of our actions will be informed by that love.

These same theologians provide various categories to help identify the movement of conversion, such as affective, moral, or religious conversion. Before reviewing these categories, keep in mind these three cautions: (1) The categories are limiting in that human life cannot be so easily compartmentalized. Western culture tends to lean toward neat dissections of the human person into various categories, as if we could understand our affect apart from our physical environment or bodily reactions. The categories do, however, provide a way of exploring a particular facet of life. This is helpful as long as we see each facet in relationship to the whole. (2) Authentic conversion manifests itself through the consistent transformation of all levels of human living, not just some (especially the "religious" levels). How we view the world cannot but affect how we love and live in the world, and how we choose to grapple with issues. Radical inconsistency in the various facets of our lives should give us clues as to areas of resistance to the movement of grace. (3) The Tradition provides criteria for evaluating conversion, such as the fruits of the Spirit cited in Galatians 5:22–23 or the embracing of the life-style of the beatitudes in Matthew 5:3–10. However, personal conversion cannot be measured against the process or journey of another. The journey of conversion is not about competition but about authentic response to the love of God. We will briefly explore some of these categories of conversion.

Intellectual conversion is the shift from knowing the facts and information to knowing what is going on when one knows and understands. In effect, it is the willingness to critically grapple with the information (is it real? is it true?) rather than simply accepting the facts because they are presented as such. Intellectual acquisition (just knowing the facts) can lead to uncritical idealism or one-dimensional thinking.

Moral conversion concerns itself with the radical recentering of how we make choices and decisions. It is the restructuring of moral decision-making from that based on what satisfies the individual (or even a society) to decision-making rooted in values. Many people assume that their decisions are value-based. However, often this is convenience-values, i.e., values that are consistent with what satisfies the individual. Moral conversion is exhibited when one consistently makes choices based on values, even when the choices mean sacrificing personal gain for the sake of true values (e.g., authentic self-sacrifice).

Affective conversion is the movement and recognition from a simplistic view of affectivity to an acceptance of the complexity of feelings. For example, someone remains in control in all situations, thereby effectively blocking affectivity and any appropriate response. Or, in a state of explosion, loses control of him or herself and responds with inappropriate feeling. Both examples can lead to affective atrophy: the hardening of the heart. Someone else is able to grapple with the complexity of emotions that emerge in life situations, and appropriately choose a response consistent both with the actual feeling and the situation.

Religious conversion is a shift from living life as a puzzle or set of problems we endure to accepting a religious worldview, i.e., a genuine openness to value in all of its manifestations leading to a sense of life as mystery and gift. Religious conversion leads to a life of hope rather than a life of despair.

Theistic conversion is the reordering of our perceptions and attitudes from one that acknowledges an Ultimate Force that directs the universe (usually an impersonal energy or force) to a manner of living rooted in both a personal and communal relationship with the creator God. In the Christian community, the contours of theistic conversion are shaped by our understanding of Christianity, the church, and the gospel.

Christian conversion is the shift from acknowledgment of the historical Jesus (or, in the other direction, of the Superstar Christ) to a recognition of God's love for all of us made flesh in the risen Christ. Ecclesial conversion is a shift from living with the church as "they"—an institution—to church as a living community of faith. Gospel conversion is the shift from focusing on gaining one's personal salvation to embracing a commitment to the mission of the reign of God.

Exercise: Exploring the Landscape

• *Return to the opening exercise of this chapter. In a few sentences, describe the conversion that was happening in that story.*

CONVERSION SHIFTS

Type	From	To
INTELLECTUAL	Knowing the facts and information; idealism	Critical knowledge and critical realism
MORAL	Self-satisfaction as criteria of choices	Values as criteria of choices
AFFECTIVE	Inability to express true feelings; atrophy	Ability to accept and express true feelings
RELIGIOUS	Living life as a puzzle or set of problems	Accepting religious worldview: genuine openness to value in all of its manifestations
THEISTIC	An Ultimate Force that directs the universe (usually impersonal)	Personal and communal relationship with the Creator God
CHRISTIAN	Historical Jesus (or the Superstar Christ)	God's love made flesh in the risen Christ.
ECCLESIAL	The church as "they," an institution	The church as community of faith
GOSPEL	Gaining one's personal salvation	Embracing a commitment to the mission of the reign of God

Figure 3

_____

_____

_____

_____

• *What particular dimensions of conversion (e.g., religious, moral, intellectual) were affected at that time?*

_____

_____

_____

• Choose one of those dimensions and write out the shift in landscape that occurred. For example: "Moral: I realize that I was pretty selfish when it came to planning our schedules. I shifted from selfishness to recognizing the needs of someone else."

_____

_____

_____

_____

_____

Conversion Stories in Scripture

The Hebrew and Christian scriptures are filled with stories of conversion, of individuals and communities who return to life with God. Hopefully, it is now clearer that the journey of conversion is an integral part of the disciple-making process. This has been consistent throughout our tradition.

The Order chooses three particular stories of conversion to focus catechumens and the rest of the church on God's call to the fullness of life. These stories, heard every year during the celebration of the scrutinies in Lent are: the woman at the well (John 4:5–42), the man born blind (John 9:1–41), and the raising of Lazarus (John 11:1–45). In Chapter 4 you will have an opportunity to pray those texts for yourself. For now, let us explore the particular focus on conversion each story opens for us.

Conversion: Facing the Truth (The woman at the well)

Conversion is what is done to us by God that allows the possibility of full humanity to emerge, not what we do for God. In the protection of our security—however we name it: self-sufficiency, fear, control, isolation, success at all costs—we boldly walk to the well of life only to encounter life-giving water that is freely given but that will also demand of us confrontation with our truth—and our personal evil— and surrender of it for forgiveness and freedom. Such surrender has a cost: a restored life-style, a return to authentic living with others, and the offering of this gift of freedom to others. The cost is a new way of being in love.

• *Do you want to risk drinking from a new well, one that will change you?*

_____

_____

Conversion: Confronting Systemic Evil (The man born blind)

The call of conversion affects not only the individual, but the very systems and institutions we live in. These systems are often bigger than we are, and yet can draw us into inauthentic living because of the forceful attraction of power, wealth, and control. Such systemic evil disconnects the human community rather than drawing it together. Such evil is larger than our individual choices; yet we contribute to its growth and pervasiveness by our refusal to see truth and to acknowledge the bankruptcy of those systems that are not life-giving and life-sustaining. It is easier to exploit the weak, the marginal, the different. The Light of the World shatters the darkness of such blindness and lights a new path. If we allow this new light to expose the darkness of sin in our lives and in the very structures and systems we support, the possibility of new vision with the promise of renewed possibility can emerge. But the cost will mean exposing the comfortable ways that keep us in sin: not just the obvious unjust structures or oppressive regimes, but the subtle (and often "religious") ways of living that exclude, oppress, and deny life to those who don't fit in. The ways of love undo the structures of sin and evil.

• *Can we bear the light?*

_____

_____

Conversion: Life Over Death (The raising of Lazarus)

The power of evil is greater than our choices for evil, although our personal and communal choices contribute to the moral surd, the drag on human authenticity. The raising of Lazarus makes a claim on us to accept and witness to the power of the Christ risen in our midst. It is the ultimate proclamation of belief: we place our hearts, our very lives, on the redemption of the cosmos. The raising of Lazarus prefigures for us the resurrection of Jesus, the Christ. Christ's resurrection heralds the destiny of the rest of the world community. With a strong and vital sense of reality, we stand firm with hope. This means naming death in all of its forms—personally, spiritually, communally, politically, environmentally. This means recognizing all that binds people's hearts and lives, keeping them enslaved. This means standing as a people at the energy center of the universe—the cross—knowing that true power is the gift of the Spirit. The triumph of grace in all of its cosmic dimensions awakens and conforms us into the Christ for the world. Such true love is the heart of authentic conversion of individuals and communities, structures and institutions, and the very cosmos.

• *Do we want to be unbound and set free?*

_____

_____

• *Will we allow the power of grace to send us to unbind and set free?*

_____

_____

The Sponsor as Companion in Conversion

It is helpful to remember that conversion is a shift from one way of life to another —from isolation to relationship, from fear to hope. Within this fundamental restructuring, there are ongoing levels or strata of movement. To help illustrate this, look at the experience of human love. At first, there is the radical reordering of life: We fall in love and nothing seems the same because of it. Over time, that love

deepens, intensifies, is purified. We experience the development of our love relationship, making commitments, struggling through fidelity and the like. But all of
that is still rooted in a fundamental decision of love. The same is true with God.

Such restructuring of life—the result of true conversion—elicits various responses, especially in the early stages: doubt, fear, loss of control, elation, sorrow,
excitement, anticipation. The sponsor is one who walks with the catechumen or
candidate without talking away the experience. While good communication skills
will be helpful, there are a few attitudes a sponsor can choose that will be invaluable
in walking this journey of conversion with another.

Reflected on own terrain:

Becoming more aware of one's own conversion journey will help a sponsor
empathize with a catechumen or candidate. Although the particulars will differ
from person to person, there is a basic pattern to the conversion journey: setting
out, disruption, period of confusion and assessment, restructuring, and living it
out. The setting out refers to the period immediately prior to the conversion experience: things begin to feel somewhat uncomfortable, a bit off center, or there is a
sense of dissatisfaction. The disruption occurs at some point: things are no longer
what they seem. What worked before just doesn't work for you now. Perhaps it is
experienced as crisis, or something more subtle. However it is experienced, there is
a significant shift or change happening. This is followed by a period of confusion
and assessment. What is going on? Why is this happening to me? What is happening to me? What do I really want, need? The crisis of inquiry leads (presuming one
is still open to new possibilities) to a restructuring: there is no going back to the way
things were. Now there is something new, you are new. Perhaps it is difficult to put
the experience into words, but you know there has been a shift. And now you are
given the choice of living in this new way, allowing the restructuring to inform your
future choices. Or you can refuse the change and try to live as if nothing has
happened—except something *has* happened.

Exercise: Knowing the Terrain

*• Recall a significant moment in your conversion journey. Try to reflect on the
experience in terms of the movements of conversion.*
• Setting out:

_____

_____

_____

_____

_____

• *Disruption:*

_____

_____

_____

_____

• *Period of confusion and assessment:*

_____

_____

_____

_____

_____

• *Restructuring:*

_____

_____

_____

_____

_____

• *Living it out:*

_____

_____

_____

_____

_____

Comfortable with the confusion:

The journey of conversion is not an easy one. The tendency of some sponsors will be to try to cover up the uncomfortable parts of the journey, or dismiss away those feelings so the catechumen will be comfortable. That would be such a disservice to the catechumen. Sponsors need to allow the catechumen to experience the various dimensions of the conversion journey, the periods of delight as well as the periods of pain. Sponsors are not there to save catechumens from these experiences, but rather to walk with them on this rugged terrain, perhaps helping to hold a lamp to their feet.

Exercise: Remembering the Confusion

• *Return to your conversion story from the last exercise. Jot down the various feelings you experienced throughout each of the periods of the conversion moment.*

_____

_____

_____

No need to fix it:

In addition to allowing the catechumen to live in the confusion, sponsors need to relinquish their desire to fix the situation, to make everything better. As mentioned earlier, this would be a disservice. Instead, sponsors remain as faithful companions, witnessing through their presence that new life emerges from the pain of conversion. This is not to suggest that sponsors should be supporting destructive painful patterns of the catechumens, such as self-abasement, willful neglect, shaming, or unhealthy guilt. Sponsors, learning from their experience and with the aid of members of the pastoral staff, help catechumens discern the difference between pain that brings growth and pain that destroys.

Exercise: Learning from the Pain

• *Continuing with your conversion story, choose one particularly painful moment in the journey. Describe that moment:*

_____

_____

_____

_____

_____

• *Having come through the experience, what did you learn about yourself, others, and God from that experience?*

_____

_____

_____

_____

_____

Sensitive to the Spirit:

Sponsors need to be mindful throughout the conversion journey that the motivation and fruit of conversion is God's gracious love. A journey that brings bitterness and destruction is not part of the work of God. Additionally, sponsors need to help catechumens experience the depth of the conversion experience, allowing it time to ferment and produce the new wine of changed lives. Thus, while there will be times of charged emotions, it is safe to say that extremes of emotion are to be acknowledged but not used as criteria for discerning the conversion journey.

Exercise:

• *Jot down the major feelings experienced throughout the conversion moment identified above.*

_____

_____

_____

• *Circle the feelings that were very intense and short-lived.*
• *What were the consistent feelings that carried you throughout the conversion moment?*

_____

_____

_____

• *Compare this list with the feelings you circled above.*
• *Based on your experience, what insight do you have regarding conversion and emotions?*

_____

_____

_____

_____

_____

Exercise: Sharing in the Conversion Story

• *Spend time with your catechumen or candidate and begin to talk about the conversion journey in his or her life.*
• *What brought him or her to your parish community?*

_____

_____

_____

• *What keeps him or her in this process?*

_____

_____

_____

• *What does he or she hope will happen in his or her life because of life within this community?*

_____

_____

_____

3

The Ministry
of Sponsor

Introduction

Most of us learn something new—a skill, some knowledge, a way of life—from others who already are somewhat familiar with the material. In such periods of apprenticeship, there is often someone in particular who is delegated to assume some level of responsibility with the learner. The establishment of that relationship is akin to sponsorship.

A sponsor in any organization is a person who serves as a companion and guide to someone new to the organization. Additionally, the sponsor provides the organization with the appropriate reassurances that the candidate is, indeed, a worthwhile candidate for membership.

Contemporary forms of sponsorship vary. For example: (1) sponsoring someone on a Food Walk; (2) sponsoring someone at work; (3) sponsoring someone in a club or organization; (4) sponsoring someone in a support group (such as Alcoholics Anonymous); (5) sponsoring someone in a religious setting (such as a church). What they all have in common is the willingness of the sponsor to invest in the other person in some way. They differ in the style and degree of that investment. For example, sponsorship for a Food Walk usually takes the form of monetary and moral support, whereas sponsorship in Alcoholics Anonymous requires a personal investment of care, support, and time to the new member. Sponsors in A.A. commit themselves, based on their experience of being sponsored through sobriety, to being available at all times for the new member who struggles with the issues—emotional and physical—of chemical dependence.

Exercise: The Experience of Sponsorship

• *As you presently understand your role, how would you define what being a sponsor means?*

_____

_____

_____

_____

_____

• *I consider these skills important for the ministry of sponsor:*

• _____

• _____

• _____

• _____

• _____

• *The strengths I bring to this ministry are:*

• _____

• _____

• _____

• _____

• _____

• *What I need to be a better sponsor is:*

• _____

• _____

• _____

• _____

• _____

Maintenance or Sacramental Sponsorship

As with the various experiences of sponsoring in our culture, there are levels or styles of sponsorship in the church: (1) financial sponsors; (2) sponsorship into parish groups or organizations; (3) sacramental sponsorship. Financial sponsorship takes various forms: weekly donations, regular tithing, special collections, planned giving, special campaigns such as the church building fund. Sponsorship into parish groups usually requires the sponsor to provide minimal exposure to the workings of the group, explain the procedures and expectations of the group, and be a good and supportive ear as one becomes assimilated into the group.

Sacramental sponsorship is different from these other forms of sponsorship. Unfortunately for most Catholics, their understanding of sponsoring is limited to one of the two above, even when it comes to sacramental sponsorship. The other forms of sponsorship mentioned, while requiring some level of personal investment, are usually maintenance forms of sponsorship. That is, they provide the necessary basics, such as money or presence at meetings, without always exacting life-style commitments. Of course, there are exceptions to that. People who are committed to tithing, for example, do that within the larger context of their understanding of their commitment to the community. But by and large, most members of the parish experience maintenance sponsorship rather than sacramental sponsorship.

To help clarify this, let's look at some typical examples of sponsoring for sacramental celebrations: infant baptism, confirmation, and marriage. It is quite common that the sponsor for infant baptism—the godparent—is usually a relative or friend of the family chosen for this role precisely because they are family or friend. However appropriate that might be, it would be fair to venture that most godparents at infant baptism have a better understanding of their role to provide for the infant if the parents should die rather than modeling a Christian life-style, along with the parents, to help mentor the child into discipleship. The awareness of the sponsor's responsibility to the community to help provide these foundations for the child is also usually absent.

Sponsorship in the sacrament of confirmation has moved from one anonymous person standing for all the candidates to one very similar to the role of sponsor in baptism. In fact, it is encouraged that the sponsor at confirmation be the same as the sponsor at baptism to highlight the intimate link between these two initiation sacraments. Many parishes require more direct involvement of sponsors in the preparation process for confirmation, and are beginning to make the bridge from maintenance sponsorship to sacramental sponsorship.

The third example, marriage, shares many similarities to infant baptism. The sponsoring role is assumed by the witnesses (commonly called the "best man" and "maid/matron of honor"). As with infant baptism, these persons are chosen because of their friendship, which on one level is appropriate. But for sacramental sponsorship in marriage, the sponsors need to be part of the discerning of readiness to celebrate the sacrament and willing to give testimony on behalf of both the couple and the community of the appropriateness of this celebration. Unfortunately, the decorative trappings of the ceremony take priority over the sacramental dimensions.

A second level of sponsorship—the sponsorship of the community—is often lacking in these sacramental celebrations. Or, at best, is there in some tacit form. Sacraments are the prayers of the community, not only the individuals celebrating. Until we reestablish the foundations and roots of sacramental celebration in the community by celebrating them consistently with the community, we will have difficulties developing the layers of sacramental sponsorship. Our common practice of celebrating sacraments outside the context of the community—infant baptism on Sunday afternoon, marriage on Saturday afternoon with the invited guests, first eucharist or confirmation at special celebrations that can only accommodate the candidates and their immediate families—needs to shift to place sacramental celebrations back into the normative life of the community. For most communities, that is the Sunday assembly.

With the implementation of the Order of Christian Initiation of Adults, we discover a renewal of the ministry of sponsor that is more akin to sacramental sponsorship rather than maintenance sponsorship. One of the significant contributions of the Order is the retrieval of this important ministry and its potential implications for sponsorship in other sacraments.

Exercise: Sponsor Clarification

• *Write an example from your experience of maintenance sponsorship.*

_____

_____

_____

_____

_____

• *Define maintenance sponsorship.*

_____

_____

_____

_____

• *Write an example from your experience of sacramental sponsorship.*

_____

_____

_____

_____

_____

• *Define sacramental sponsorship.*

_____

_____

_____

_____

• *What are some of the key differences or distinctions between the two?*

_____

_____

_____

_____

• *What do you need at this point to help you better understand your role as a sacramental sponsor?*

_____

_____

_____

Sponsoring in the Order of Christian Initiation of Adults

Sponsoring in initiation has two aspects: personal sponsoring and communal sponsoring. Both are necessary and interact with each other on a regular basis. In fact, personal sponsorship is rooted in the community's role as primary sponsor for the candidate.

For a fuller picture of the ministry of sponsor, let's look at the role of sponsor in the early church. Usually, someone was drawn to the Christian way of life by the example and life-style of Christians. Curious, one would approach Christians, seeking whatever they had that caused their lives to be different. After careful scrutiny of the motives of the inquirer, the Christian brought the inquirer to the assembly of Christians. The inquirer was welcomed by the church and enrolled in a long process of preparation for full initiation into the community. The Christian who brought the inquirer to the community—or someone else delegated from the community—was charged with the responsibility of serving as a companion and friend to the inquirer throughout the preparation. Together they conversed about the Lord Jesus, his way of life, the community of believers, the need to change one's life, prayer, some of the practices of the community, and the like. Over the course of years, the catechumen was gradually introduced into the Christian life-style by the community and, in particular, the sponsor. The sponsor witnessed to the community regarding the conversion of the catechumen, and accompanied the catechumen during ritual celebrations. When the catechumen became a member of the faithful at the celebration of the sacraments, the sponsor was present. And together, the neophyte and sponsor grew in their friendship and relationship as members of the order of the faithful.

Today, the ministry of the sponsor is as essential as in the early community. Such ministry is rooted in the vision of ministry provided in the ritual text that is both fresh yet ancient. This vision of ministry is a retrieval of the fundamental beliefs that: (a) All are called by baptism to mission and service for the reign of God; (b) Charisms are given by God to all; (c) The proper ordering of the church comes when all the charisms are used for the building up of the body of Christ; (d) The responsibility of initiation, then, rests with all the baptized; (e) Within this communal responsibility and sponsorship, there is a differentiation of ministries:

bishop, presbyter, sponsor, catechist, liturgist, and the like. Sponsorship comes from that vision of church and ministry. It is not just the activity of someone to "get more members." It is a much more radical vision.

Qualities of Sponsoring

Most people hesitate about assuming the responsibility of sponsor because they feel intimidated or unworthy. While there are certain qualities for sponsoring, they really do not differ from those qualities the community expects of all the fully initiated. The sponsor, as a member of the order of faithful, serves as companion, guide, and learner in the Christian way of life. Sponsors are not academic theologians, nor extraordinary mystics or saints. In fact, the primary qualification is participation in the ordinary life of the order of the faithful. And it is precisely as members of the order of the faithful that we discover ourselves as theologians, mystics, and saints.

Sponsors freely enter into serious relationships—with themselves, the church, and the catechumens. Sponsoring is not maintenance-oriented. Rather, sponsors are willing to invest themselves with and for the other. At the same time, sponsors recognize that much of what happens is the work of grace that they participate in.

Sponsors desire to share their faith and belief with the catechumens. They are willing to risk and express what is sacred in their lives and the life of the community, knowing that faith is fostered and nurtured not by facts but by the lived stories and beliefs of the community. Sponsors also recognize there are things about the community's faith they are not completely familiar with, and are willing to say that. They are also willing, when necessary, to do the work that needs to be done to find out some particular fact or clarify an issue. And they are willing to help the catechumen learn how to find these answers rather than merely providing answers.

Sponsors are willing to be available. They have a fundamental stance of openness to receive the gifts of God that are given through the encounter with another, in this situation, the catechumen. Such receptivity can only happen when it is balanced by availability: of time, of hospitality, of care.

These same qualities are exhibited in maturing communities of the order of the faithful: relational, interrelated rather than dependent, sharing of faith and belief, sincere inquiry, appropriate study, availability, and generosity. The ministry of sponsor, in many ways, serves as a focus for life in the order of the faithful. Initiation is about mentoring people into the life-style of the Christian disciple. It is appropriate, therefore, that the sponsors come from the ordinary life of the disciple.

Throughout this resource, you will be told that the purpose of the resource is to help make more intentional the skills and gifts that you already possess. Sponsorship is intentional activity. It highlights what is normative for a Christian community regarding the way we live and embrace the demands of discipleship. The radical nature of sponsorship—indeed, for the entire process of initiation—is the evangelizing and renewing effect it can (and does) have on our communities to embrace more fully their responsibilities.

Expectation of Sponsors in Initiation

There are certain concrete expectations a parish community has of its sponsors involved in initiation. Following are some minimal expectations of sponsoring that will need to be supplemented by your sponsor coordinator to include the particulars of your parish community.

Participate in weekly gatherings with catechumens:

Sponsors need to be present with the inquirers, catechumens and candidates for their weekly gatherings. During the period of the catechumenate, sponsors can join with the catechumens and team after the dismissal of the faithful at the end of mass. Sponsors need to be disciplined, however, to remember that their participation in these gatherings is for the primary benefit of the catechumens and candidates. Sometimes the focus turns exclusively to the issues of the sponsors to the neglect of the needs of the catechumens.

The day and time of gatherings in our parish are:

_____

_____

Meet regularly with catechumen during the week:

In addition to the parish weekly gathering, sponsors need to be in regular contact with catechumens and candidates. Often, this is the time the catechumen feels free to talk about issues or confusions. Given the normal course of relationships, sponsors will need to gradually build such a relationship with the catechumen in order for the catechumen to feel free to ask questions and talk about the faith. These regular gatherings can be a time to share prayer and insights on the scriptures, as well as provide opportunities for social contact with other members of the community. Each sponsor-catechumen relationship will need to determine how often they want to meet.

Usually, we will get together:

_____

_____

Attend sponsor formation gatherings:

Sponsor formation gatherings help sponsors become more intentional with the skills they already possess in order to serve in this important ministry. More importantly, however, these gatherings give sponsors an opportunity to talk together about their experiences as sponsors, gaining support and insight from each other.

The schedule of sponsor formation meetings for our parish is:

_____

_____

_____

_____

_____

Introduce catechumen to others in the parish community:

Individuals learn to live with a community by embracing the values of the community as exhibited in the people of the community. The community can chart out all of its teachings and values, but the ones that will be readily embraced are the ones lived by the community. Sponsors immerse catechumens and candidates into the ordinary life of the community by introducing them to people from the community. The goal of initiation is not to create new communities of people but integration into renewed communities. Introducing catechumens to members of the community, therefore, is more than exchanging greetings. It involves spending time together, perhaps in parishioners' homes.

List some members of the parish you want to introduce to your catechumen:

_____

_____

_____

_____

_____

Invite catechumen to parish functions:

As with meeting members of the parish, catechumens need to be exposed to the normal life of the parish community: socials, service work, organizations, small groups, and the like. Sponsors are careful to expose the catechumen to the richness of parish life.

Parish activities we plan to participate in together:

_____

_____

_____

_____

_____

Pray and share faith with catechumen:

The community and social life needs to be balanced by the sharing of faith and prayer with the catechumen. A helpful focus for such times together is the Sunday scripture readings for that particular week.

Ideas and insights from other sponsors that can aid me in praying and sharing faith with my catechumen:

_____

_____

_____

_____

_____

Spend social time with catechumen:

One of the best ways to nurture authentic relationships is to simply spend time together, enjoying each other's presence. This is usually enhanced by socializing together: movies, going shopping and the like. The key is striking a balance between social time and focused time sharing faith.

Some social events I have discovered my catechumen and I enjoy are:

_____

_____

_____

_____

_____

Help catechumen to discern God's call:

The sponsor is not there to tell the catechumen what to do or how to do it. Rather, the sponsor helps the catechumen to listen to what is happening, both inside and outside. That is discernment: truly listening to what is happening and making appropriate choices based on that. In order to help catechumens discern

God's will and call, sponsors need to regularly evaluate the movement of God's spirit in their own lives.

At this time of my life, my discernment of God's call is:

_____

_____

_____

_____

_____

Share information with catechumen about the Catholic faith:

Often there will be basic questions about the Catholic faith, and the catechumen will come to the sponsor with those questions. As mentioned earlier, the sponsor is not intended to be an academic theologian. Together, the sponsor and catechumen can carefully explore answers to basic questions. Sponsors will need to know the resources available to them (such as the parish Director of Religious Education, the Pastor, or a parish library) to aid them.

Parish Resources available to me (and phone numbers) are:

_____

_____

_____

_____

_____

Take time for my own personal enrichment and formation as a disciple:

Sponsors can help immerse catechumens into a Christian way of life best by their own immersion in that life. This would include prayer, study, reflection, and community life (both social and liturgical). Many sponsors find Bible study and prayer groups helpful supports to them in this ministry.

Currently, dimensions of my own enrichment include:

_____

_____

_____

_____

_____

Discuss any concerns with the coordinator of sponsors:

Sponsors discover very early that their ministry is not done in isolation: it is supported by the community at large, other sponsors, and the coordinator of sponsors. It is the particular ministry of the coordinator to "sponsor the sponsors." The coordinator of sponsors is available to the sponsors to respond to particular questions, help discern needs, and the like. Sponsors need to keep in regular contact with the sponsor coordinator.

Address and phone number of our parish coordinator of sponsors:

_____

_____

Each parish community will also have particular expectations of their sponsors which they have discussed before the sponsors have committed themselves to their ministry.

List any other explicit expectations of sponsors in your parish community:

_____

_____

_____

_____

_____

Are there any particular questions or concerns you have now that you want to address with your sponsor coordinator? If so, list them here, leaving space for his or her feedback to you.

_____

_____

_____

_____

_____

_____

_____

_____

What Is a Godparent?

Many parishes make clear the distinction between sponsor and godparent. Sponsors come from the parish community to represent the community during the process of preparation for sacramental initiation. Usually sponsor-catechumen matchings are chosen in the name of the parish by the coordinator of sponsors. Godparents are chosen because of their witness to the Christian life, character, and level of friendship with the catechumen. The godparent must be a fully initiated member of the Catholic Church—a person fully initiated in another Christian denomination may serve as a godparent as long as there is also a fully initiated Catholic as a godparent. Because the role of godparent is more than a ceremonial function, indeed it is a commitment of lifelong friendship in the Lord, the choice and formation of godparents needs to be given the same level of consideration as with sponsors. The popular practice of requesting people to serve as godparents for our children based on purely social or obligatory reasons has contributed to the functioning of godparents as purely ceremonial witnesses.

Godparents assume their ritual role during the rite of election. Many parishes, however, continue the active role of sponsors at this time as well. Some people, in fact, choose their parish sponsor to serve as their godparent as well.

Exercise: Self-Evaluation of Sponsoring

• *If you are a new sponsor, return to this activity after you have had a chance to serve as a sponsor. If you have been serving as a sponsor, review the basic expectations of sponsoring listed below and rate your level of service, using the following scale:*

   1 = Never
   2 = Rarely
   3 = Sometimes
   4 = Usually
   5 = Always

• *After each basic expectation, there is space provided for you to write concrete actions you can take to strengthen your service in this particular area.*

Participate in weekly gatherings with catechumens: *1   2   3   4   5*

_____

_____

_____

Meet regularly with catechumen during the week: *1   2   3   4   5*

_____

_____

_____

Attend sponsor formation gatherings: 1   2   3   4   5

_____

_____

_____

Introduce catechumen to others in the parish community: 1   2   3   4   5

_____

_____

_____

Invite catechumen to parish functions: 1   2   3   4   5

_____

_____

_____

Pray and share faith with catechumen: 1   2   3   4   5

_____

_____

_____

Spend social time with catechumen: 1   2   3   4   5

_____

_____

_____

Help catechumen to discern God's call: *1 2 3 4 5*

_____

_____

_____

Share information with catechumen about the Catholic   *1 2 3 4 5*
faith:

_____

_____

_____

Take time for my own personal enrichment and formation   *1 2 3 4 5*
as a disciple:

_____

_____

_____

Discuss any concerns with the coordinator of sponsors: *1 2 3 4 5*

_____

_____

_____

4

Celebrating Initiation: The Role of Sponsors

Introduction

Sponsors play an active part throughout the process of Christian initiation. In addition to participating in the weekly gatherings with the catechumens and candidates, sponsors serve as guides, companions and witnesses for the public rituals of the Order of Christian Initiation of Adults.

This chapter will explore the role of sponsors in each of the periods and stages of the Order. Because the rites will be adapted for each pastoral situation, this chapter will only provide the broad strokes of responsibility. After each period and stage there is space provided for the sponsor to write in particular instructions and responsibilities for his or her parish community.

Period of the Precatechumenate

During the period of the precatechumenate, those inquiring into the life of the Catholic Christian community will gather with the precatechumenate team to explore basic questions and issues with an eye to discerning their readiness and willingness to embrace the demands of discipleship within the Roman Catholic Christian community. Sponsors are an important part of this process.

Usually sponsors are invited to participate in the precatechumenate gatherings.

In this way, before the matching of sponsors with candidates, everyone has an opportunity to meet and spend time together in a comfortable setting. Sponsors are encouraged to share their own stories of faith and conversion with the candidates. Eventually, sponsors and candidates will begin to establish a one-on-one relationship that will continue throughout the rest of the preparation process. The procedure for establishing this relationship will differ from parish to parish. Some parishes wait to see if sponsor-candidate pairings naturally emerge. Others assign the sponsor to accompany a particular candidate. Usually, it is a combination of both: a sense of the right chemistry mixed with an awareness of the needs of the candidates and the particular gifts of a sponsor.

The formal sponsor-candidate relationship needs to happen early enough in the precatechumenate so a relationship can begin to form before any of the public ritual celebrations. Thus, during this period, the sponsor will want to be sensitive to the dynamics of forming a new relationship, being careful to keep in mind that people grow in relationships at various paces. Slowly, however, is generally a good pace to grow together. In addition to being present at precatechumenate gatherings, the sponsor begins to invite the candidate to other parish functions, or simply to get together during the week for coffee or a meal. The intent is not to overwhelm but to welcome gently through warm and genuine hospitality.

Along with the precatechumenate team, sponsors begin to share their own stories and the stories of the community, thus welcoming the inquirers into telling their own stories. As stories are told, the inquirers begin to correlate their story with the big story of the Christian tradition, discovering how the Christian story can and does bring meaning to people's lives.

The adventure of storytelling is deepened and enhanced by the ongoing process of questioning. Initially, inquirers will come with basic questions about the church, its policies or practices. Sponsors can be helpful here, providing basic answers. But as the storytelling deepens, accompanied by other activities provided by the precatechumenate team, the kinds of questions asked by the inquirers shift from questions of information to questions of meaning. Sponsors need to avoid the temptation of trying to answer these questions. Rather, sponsors invite the inquirers' questions, exploring their possible meanings and the eventual new questions that emerge. Questions about life's meaning and mystery are never fully answered.

Specific information about the precatechumenate in your parish community.

_____

Rite of Acceptance into the Order of Catechumens

Parish communities celebrate the rite of acceptance at various times during the year, thus enabling inquirers to take the time needed to discern readiness to enter into the formal process of formation and celebration of discipleship. While the decision to celebrate the rite rests primarily with the candidates (in consultation with the initiation team), the sponsors contribute to this discernment process.

Discerning readiness:

In preparing for this discernment, sponsors review what the Order of Christian Initiation of Adults says about readiness for the rite of acceptance:

> The prerequisite for making this first step is that the beginnings of the spiritual life and the fundamentals of Christian teaching have taken root in the candidates. Thus there must be evidence of first faith that was conceived during the period of evangelization and precatechumenate and of an initial conversion and intention to change their lives and to enter into a relationship with God in Christ. Consequently, there must also be evidence of the first stirrings of repentance, a start of the practice of calling upon God in prayer, a sense of the Church, and some experience of the company and spirit of Christians through contact with a priest or with members of the community. The candidate should also be instructed about the celebration of the liturgical rite of acceptance (*RCIA*, n. 42).

Using that text as a guide, the sponsor assists the candidate to discern readiness.

Discernment is the process of actively listening to God's call by being attentive to one's interior and exterior world. In a prayerful posture, and aided by a companion, one listens to the heart to get a sense of one's inner stirrings in order to get a clearer sense of direction. Thus, one is attentive to thoughts, images, feelings, attitudes and hopes. One also listens to the exterior world, such as insights from others, changed behaviors, scripture, other readings, and guidance from respected companions. Both dimensions are essential for discernment. The goal of the discernment process is to come to a more authentic sense of self in relationship with the community: What is the right fit?

The sponsor, while supporting the inquirer as he or she searches the interior world, can help assess the exterior world. By using the criteria established by the rite, the sponsor can suggest questions for further reflection to round out the discernment. Sponsors need to be careful to recognize that discernment of readiness is not the same as asking: "Has the candidate met the requirements?" One cannot earn sacraments; they are not rewards for superior moral lives or the acquisition of certain knowledge. The criterion for celebration of all the rites of the Order of Christian Initiation of Adults—indeed, of all sacraments—is not what one has done and accumulated (such as information) but rather one who has discovered him or herself to be in relationship to God and the community and how this celebration articulates that relationship. That is why the celebration of the rite sets the criteria for all that precedes and not vice versa.

• *Gather with other sponsors and create questions that will begin a discussion between candidates and sponsors for each of the areas for discernment for the rite of acceptance (refer to RCIA, n. 42).*

a) *Beginnings of the spiritual life have taken root:*

_____

_____

_____

b) *Fundamentals of Christian teaching have taken root:*

_____

_____

_____

c) *Evidence of first faith:*

_____

_____

_____

d) *Evidence of initial conversion and intent to change one's life:*

_____

_____

_____

e) *Evidence of a desire to enter into relationship with God:*

_____

_____

_____

f) *Evidence of the first stirrings of repentance:*

_____

_____

_____

g) *Start of the practice of calling God in prayer:*

_____

_____

_____

h) Sense of the church:

_____

_____

_____

i) Some experience of the company and spirit of Christians:

_____

_____

_____

• *After developing some questions, refine the questions as much as possible, avoiding the check-list approach. Perhaps some of the questions can be grouped together.*

_____

_____

_____

_____

• *Following are some questions sponsors can ask of themselves during this discernment:*

1. What are concrete ways I have come to know this candidate as someone who is truly seeking the way of the life of Jesus, the Christ?

_____

_____

_____

_____

_____

2. What can I share with the community of faith to indicate to them the seriousness with which this candidate embraces this commitment?

_____

_____

_____

_____

_____

After the decision has been made to celebrate the rite of acceptance, the parish community usually provides a period of prayer and reflection (day of recollection) for the candidates and sponsors. During this time together, sponsors will help the candidates respond to two basic questions: What is it you ask of God? What is it you ask of this community? Through a slow and prayerful discussion, the candidates need to be given the opportunity to express their responses to these or similar questions in their own words.

Immediate preparation for the rite:

Before the celebration of the rite of acceptance, the sponsors will have an opportunity to review the rite and to "walk through" the ritual to be comfortable with the movement of the rite. Many parishes have stopped rehearsing the rites with candidates, realizing that the power of the rituals are enhanced when people are allowed to experience them fresh. The sponsor, therefore, becomes a key person for the celebration as he or she guides the candidate through the rite.

Sponsors will also need to prepare introductory comments about the candidates they are sponsoring so they can present the candidates to the community. If there is to be a presentation of a cross to the candidates, the sponsors will need to have them before the rite.

Sponsors will need to be with the candidates just before the rite (and hopefully, in conversation these last days before the rite). Their presence and support now is encouraging and necessary for the candidates.

Celebrating the rite of acceptance:

The community will gather inside while the sponsors and candidates remain outside of the church. The candidates will probably be nervous and curious now— the calming presence of sponsors who support and encourage is invaluable at these moments of waiting. This would be a good time to talk again about the importance of this day and how grateful this community is to the candidates for choosing to respond so generously at this time. This would also be a good time to let the candidates know that the presider will want to know what they are seeking and how we as a Christian community can support them on this journey. Reminding them that you have already discussed this, the sponsors can invite them to reflect again on the questions: What is it you ask of God? What is it you ask of this community?

The community will come outside to greet the candidates and sponsors. After everyone has assembled outside, the presider will ask the sponsors to introduce their candidates to the community. This introduction is more than merely stating someone's name, and yet it is not extended testimony. Having built a relationship with the candidates, the sponsors can speak from their experiences of the candidates. Now is the time for storytelling to the community! Without taking a great deal of time, the sponsors can help the community come to know something about the candidates. The dialogue will then continue between the presider and the candidates. Letting the candidates feel physical support from the sponsors by a strong arm around the waist or on the shoulder is helpful throughout all the rites. The sponsors will be addressed again, asking if they are willing to help the candidates on this journey of faith. Having had the opportunity to reflect on these responsibilities, the sponsors offer their affirmation.

Parishes appropriately adapt the various rites of the Order of Christian Initiation of Adults to meet the specific needs of the community. This is one of those times. Your parish may choose at this time to return to the worship space and continue with the liturgy of the word. If that is the case, guide your candidate to the seats reserved for you. Before the proclamation of the word, encourage your candidate to be attentive to God's word revealed in the scriptures. After the homily, the rite will resume. Other parishes will continue the rite outside and later move to the worship space for the liturgy of the word.

Whenever the remainder of the rite is celebrated, the sponsors bring their candidates to their assigned places for the signing of the body with the cross. This powerful ritual gesture reminds the candidates—and the community—that choosing discipleship in the Christian community is choosing to live under the cross. The presider usually leads the marking of the body through a prayer invocation, followed by petitions for each part of the body. As the body part is named, the sponsor marks that part of the body with a large cross. The signings need to be done boldly so everyone—candidates and community—recognize the claim that is being made. Thus, using one's thumb to mark the body is inadequate. Sponsors need to use the full palm of the hand, marking and touching the body part with a large cross. Usually, the community will sing an acclamation between each petition and the sponsors can take their time marking the body.

Following the signing of the senses, there is an optional rite of the presentation of the scriptures to the catechumens and candidates, followed by prayers of intercession. The catechumens and candidates will then be dismissed from the assembly to continue to break open their experience of the rite and the word proclaimed in the assembly. The sponsors return to their seats and continue with the prayer of the community.

After the dismissal of the faithful at the end of mass, the sponsors join the catechumenate community. This would be a good time for sponsors to stand with the catechumens and candidates at the church entrance so members of the parish can personally welcome them.

As with the other ritual experiences of the Order of Christian Initiation of Adults, it is important that sponsors spend time after the celebration of the rite of acceptance with the catechumens and candidates reflecting on the experience and how the rite empowers them. This is best done a few days after the experience when the power of the ritual has had time to seep into one's life.

Specific information about the rite of acceptance in your parish community.

_____

_____

_____

_____

_____

Period of the Catechumenate

The Order of Christian Initiation of Adults specifies four areas of formation for the period of the catechumenate: catechetical, spiritual, liturgical, and apostolic. Sponsors serve an important role of support and encouragement to the catechumens and candidates as they struggle to name the experience of God in their lives and the call to gospel living.

Catechetical:

Many parishes celebrate lectionary-based catechesis with the catechumens and candidates. After the homily each Sunday, the catechumens and candidates are dismissed from the community to continue to allow the presence of God in the word to make a claim on their lives, forming them into disciples. The dismissal of the catechumens and candidates is an act of hospitality by the community. Until they are welcomed to share at the table of the eucharist, we send them forth to continue to share in the real presence of Christ in the word. Sponsors join the catechumens and candidates after the dismissal of the faithful at the end of mass. If the parish has elected to continue the reflection on the scriptures and the issues of Catholic Christian living at another time, the sponsors would join with the catechumens and candidates at that time.

Sponsors will need to reflect regularly on the Sunday scriptures with the catechumens and candidates. Hopefully, this would be a rich experience of prayer and faith-sharing that happens at times other than the normal catechetical gatherings of the catechumenate. Many have found *The Catechumen's Lectionary* (Paulist Press, 1988), edited by Robert M. Hamma, to be a useful tool to begin discussion between sponsors and catechumens and candidates. In addition to providing the three-cycle lectionary of readings, a number of people experienced with initiation have provided short commentaries, prayer suggestions, and ideas for journaling that could serve as a starting point for faith-sharing between sponsors and catechumens and candidates.

Often, when catechumens and candidates have questions about particular information or practices of the church, the catechumenate team will refer them to their sponsors to discuss the questions. Sponsors can avail themselves of resources provided by the parish to help answer the questions, knowing that their role is not primarily "answer-person" but assisting the catechumen and candidates in finding ways of discovering the answers.

Spiritual:

An important dimension of spiritual development during the period of the catechumenate is the immersion of catechumens and candidates into the rich life of the community: its prayer, its service, its hospitality. The bottom line of the spiritual formation dimension of the catechumenate is the fostering and development of relationships that help the catechumens and candidates respond to the call of conversion.

Sponsors encourage this in a variety of ways: joining with the catechumens and candidates for times of prayer, sharing insights and experiences of personal prayer, inviting them to participate in activities in the parish, introducing them to members of the parish community, suggesting ways they can become more involved in the life of the parish, to name a few. Catechumens and candidates will need to deepen all these experiences by developing a personal prayer life. Sponsors can both encourage and participate in that personal prayer life as much as possible.

Liturgical:

Throughout the period of the catechumenate, there will be a variety of intensifying rites that will help ground the catechumens and candidates in the public worship of the community. These intensifying rituals—celebrations of the word of God, blessings, anointings, minor exorcisms—are often celebrated during the catechetical gatherings with the catechumens and candidates. Special occasions in the life of the parish community may also be important times to celebrate some of these rites, such as on the anniversary of the parish, or during a difficult time in the parish.

The role of sponsors during these rites is primarily one of companion, offering care and support. The specifics of the liturgical celebrations will be shared with the sponsors, as needed. The sponsors, aware of the important place of liturgical formation in the life of a Catholic Christian, can assist in helping the catechumens and candidates come to a better personal understanding of the meaning of the intensifying rites after they have been celebrated.

Apostolic:

Apostolic formation—living lives of discipleship—is not something that can be imposed from the outside. Hopefully, throughout the entire process, catechumens and candidates have been alerted to the action/service dimensions of discipleship. The sponsor can play an important role at this time. Sponsors can gently invite a more critical reflection on the role of service in the life of the Christian, and then suggest possible ways that the catechumens and candidates could explore to test their gifts of service. Sponsors can bring catechumens and candidates to participate in traditional forms of outreach in the community: working with the poor, legislative lobbying, visiting the sick, providing meals for the homebound, and the like. This would also be a good time to begin to explore other issues in the community, and how sponsors and catechumens and candidates can begin to respond: racism, sexism, discrimination against persons with handicaps, people living with AIDS, and other marginalized persons.

Sponsors need to remember that service for the sake of service, however noble and altruistic, is not what is important here. Rather, the focus is service as the way of the disciple in response to God's action and call of grace. Sponsors spend time with the catechumens and candidates reflecting on the meaning of their service.

Specific information about the catechumenate in your parish community.

_____

_____

_____

_____

_____

Rite of Election

The period of the catechumenate lasts for at least one year. During that time, the catechumens and candidates have been exposed to the life of the Catholic Christian community in a variety of ways. Furthermore, there have been changes in their lives (conversion) that have prepared them to embrace the demands of discipleship. Each year, prior to Lent, all involved in the catechumenate process begin to discern each individual's readiness to celebrate the sacraments at Easter. In this discernment process, it may become clear that some catechumens or candidates are not ready to celebrate sacraments and will continue in the period of the catechumenate.

Discerning readiness:

Unlike the rite of acceptance—which is celebrated at various times during the year—the rite of election is celebrated once a year on the First Sunday of Lent. Sponsors join the catechumens, candidates, and the initiation team in a process of discerning readiness to celebrate the Easter sacraments of initiation. The process for this discernment varies, but usually includes the sponsor and catechumen or candidate spending time together reflecting on the importance of this step. Some parishes gather the catechumens, candidates, sponsors, and team together to enter into a communal experience of discernment. At that time, the catechumens, candidates, and sponsors would share the fruit of their reflection and prayers.

In preparing for this discernment, sponsors review what the Order of Christian Initiation of Adults says about readiness for the rite of election:

> Before the rite of election is celebrated, the catechumens are expected to have undergone a conversion in mind and in action and to have developed a sufficient acquaintance with Christian teaching as well as a spirit of faith and charity. With deliberate will and an enlightened faith they must have the intention to receive the sacraments of the church, a resolve they will express publicly in the actual celebration of the rite (*RCIA*, n. 120).

Using that text as a guide—and remembering the four dimensions of this period (*RCIA*, n. 75)—the sponsor assists the catechumen or candidate to discern readiness for election.

• Gather with other sponsors, as you did for discernment for the rite of acceptance, and create questions that will begin a discussion between the catechumen or candidate and sponsor that will help facilitate the process of discernment for election. Given the broad strokes of both RCIA n. 75 and n. 120, the questions will need to be specific to the life of your faith community.

a) Conversion in mind and action:

_____

_____

b) Developed a sufficient acquaintance with Christian teaching:

_____

_____

_____

c) Developed a spirit of faith and charity:

_____

_____

_____

d) Has the intention to receive the sacraments of the church:

_____

_____

_____

• _Rework the questions, grouping those which are similar. Remember the purpose of this activity is to provide leading questions for prayer, discussion and discernment. This is not a test one takes to become Catholic._

_____

_____

_____

_____

• *Following are some questions sponsors can ask of themselves during this discernment:*

1. Can I assure this community that the catechumen or candidate I sponsor is ready to proceed toward the sacraments of initiation?

_____

_____

2. What strengths do I feel she or he offers to our community?

_____

_____

_____

3. Do I feel this catechumen or candidate is ready to minister to the community —to serve with the community by the way he or she is living the faith?

_____

_____

Immediate preparation for the rite of sending:

The presider will review the ritual celebration with the sponsors and godparents before the actual celebration. A significant piece in the ritual will be the affirmations offered by the sponsors and godparents as to the readiness of the catechumens and candidates for election. Most of us are not familiar with giving affirmations before the community; somehow, we don't associate Catholics with giving witness or testimony. And yet, the rite clearly calls for the affirmation of the sponsors, godparents, and the community as to the readiness of the catechumens and candidates for celebration of the Easter sacraments. The content of the affirmation, then, needs to reflect how the catechumens and candidates have experienced conversion in their lives. The focus is on God's action in the lives of the catechumens. These affirmations are not testimonials (such as at an awards banquet), but witnessing to God's ongoing loving presence in the life of the community through the courage and generosity of the catechumens. These affirmations are richer when they are told in story form.

Celebrating the rite of sending to election:

After the homily, the catechumens who are celebrating the rite of election are called forward, accompanied by their sponsors and godparents. The presider then requests affirmation from the sponsors and godparents about the readiness of the catechumens for election. Individually, the sponsors and godparents offer the testimony mentioned above. Further affirmations are given by members of the parish community.

The presider will invite the catechumens to sign the book of the elect while the sponsors and godparents witness the signing. Sometimes the signing of the book of the elect is celebrated at the rite of election itself.

Then the candidates for full communion are recognized by the community. As with the catechumens, the sponsors accompany the candidates and offer their affirmation, followed by spontaneous affirmations from the community. Candidates do not sign the book of the elect because it is the registry of those called to baptism. They have already been inscribed in the book of the baptized. Some parishes, however, have started the practice of inscription by candidates in a separate book.

After intercession for and prayers over the catechumens and candidates, they are dismissed to continue to break open the word with their catechist.

The affirmations by sponsors, godparents, and the parish community can be a very powerful experience for the catechumens and candidates. As in the other ritual celebrations of the Order, the sponsors and godparents are encouraged to offer physical support to the catechumens and candidates by holding them on the shoulder or around the waist.

Immediate preparation for the rite of election:

Most of the preparations for this celebration are made by the diocesan offices responsible for the implementation of the Order of Christian Initiation of Adults. Sponsors will need to make sure they know the date, time, and location of the rite of election. If the rite of sending occurs on the same day as the rite of election, the sponsors may want to spend the intervening time with the catechumens and candidates.

Celebrating the rite of election:

While the general structure of the rite of election is the same, the particular manner in which it is celebrated differs from diocese to diocese. Some dioceses prefer to celebrate the enrollment of names at the cathedral liturgy. Others request this happen at the parish rite of sending. As the Order of Christian Initiation of Adults is implemented in more and more parishes, some dioceses are celebrating regional rites of election in various parts of the diocese. Therefore, some of the elements mentioned in the rite of sending may be applicable for this celebration.

Sponsors and godparents accompany the catechumens and candidates to the site of the rite of election, and sit with them. Particular instructions for the rite will be given at the celebration itself. Usually that will include a general affirmation from all the sponsors and godparents about the readiness of the catechumens and candidates for sacramental celebration. Sometimes the catechumens and candidates will be presented to the bishop. If this happens, the sponsors and godparents normally accompany them.

The sponsors and godparents remain with the elect and candidates throughout the remainder of the rite. After the celebration, most dioceses provide some hospitality during which time sponsors and godparents can introduce the elect and candidates to the bishop.

As with the other ritual experiences of the Order, it is important that sponsors and godparents spend time after the celebration with the elect and candidates reflecting on the experience and how the rite empowers each of them. This is best done a few days after the experience when the power of the ritual has had time to seep into one's life.

Specific information about the rite of sending in your parish community and the rite of election in your diocese.

_____

_____

_____

_____

_____

Period of Purification and Enlightenment

Sponsors and godparents will recognize the changing emphasis during the period of purification and enlightenment: the focus of the period is less instructional and more reflective, akin to a retreat. The elect and candidates, although they may continue to gather with the other catechumens and candidates at the Sunday assembly, will gather separately for their breaking open of the word. This is not a time of information or catch-up. Presuming adequate and appropriate immersion in the Catholic Christian experience, this is a time to heighten and focus the experience as a preparation for sacramental celebration at Easter. The elect and candidates will celebrate rituals within the assembly that will not be celebrated by the catechumens and candidates, that is, scrutinies, penitential rite, and presentations.

Scrutinies for the Elect

Preparing for scrutinies:

The scrutinies are celebrated with the elect on the Third, Fourth, and Fifth Sundays of Lent. The primary preparation for the scrutinies usually happens through the guidance of the initiation team in a series of reflection experiences. However, sponsors and godparents help deepen the preparation by spending quality time with the elect in prayer and reflection, using the scripture texts of the scrutinies.

The first scrutiny celebrated on the Third Sunday of Lent uses the text of the woman at the well (John 4:5–42). The second scrutiny on the Fourth Sunday of Lent uses the text of the man born blind (John 9:1–41). And the third scrutiny on the Fifth Sunday of Lent uses the text of the raising of Lazarus (John 11:1–45).

• *Prior to each scrutiny, spend some time praying the gospel text for the day, writing some of your reflections.*

• *Scrutiny I: THE WOMAN AT THE WELL (John 4:5–42)—Things aren't always as they appear. Confident, capable, self-reliant. Always in control, the strong one. She approaches the well at noontime, an odd time to draw water. Most people come before the heat of the day. And as she goes for the water, she encounters one very different than herself: a man, a Jew. "Give me to drink."*

She questions, probes, challenges, protects herself. Jesus turns the tables on her. "If only you recognized God's gift." She has sight but no insight. She is still focused on herself, still protected. Jesus reaches down into her life and exposes her need for God. She then realizes that she is not in control, she could not manage this. It is all God's work. The woman slowly allows the walls of protection, fear, sin, and isolation to crumble under the gentle strength of Jesus' healing words. And she discovers meaning for her life: "I who speak to you am he (the Messiah)." Now she is outside of her preoccupation with protecting herself and inside her true identity: freed for love and compassion, justice and peace. She makes haste—she even leaves behind her jar—and goes into town (Had she not avoided them earlier? Had she, in fact, been cut off from them?) proclaiming what God has done in her life, how Jesus has turned her life around, exposing her need and meeting it with love. She shouts her story of her encounter with acceptance and forgiveness. She is changed, a new woman. Nothing can ever be the same again.

• *What is it in your life, in your community, and in the world that thirsts for living water?:*

_____

_____

_____

_____

_____

• *Scrutiny II: THE MAN BORN BLIND (John 9:1–41)—Darkness that is not chosen. Violence inflicted by others. Struggling to maneuver oneself amid both subtle and explicit exploitation. Evil, larger than oneself, that is seductive and often elusive, overwhelming yet gripping us in our gut. The man sits by the side of the road, blind from birth, experiencing the malice and condescension of many, the charity of few. He has hardened himself to their taunts and abuse. People even use his blindness to justify their lack of compassion—who's sin was it? And then someone comes along and opens his eyes, frees him from the darkness. "I am the light of the world." Nothing can be the same again—for him and for everyone else. He knows that. The others refuse to accept it, to allow the power of freedom to transform them. Instead, they attempt to keep him enslaved by their rules (mixing mud on the Sabbath!), their power struggles (they were sharply divided over Jesus), and their refusal to see (What! You are steeped in sin from your birth and you are giving us lectures!). He persists. He refuses to give in. He has been changed by a power greater than the evil that binds them. And not only is his sight restored, but he is able to see the way for his life: "Do you believe in the Son of Man? . . . I do believe." The seduction of evil and sin enslaves those who protect themselves in its illusion: "If you were blind, there would be no sin in that. But you say 'we see' and your sin remains."*

• *What is it in your life, in your community, and in the world that needs the light of Christ to dispel the darkness?*

_____

_____

_____

_____

_____

• *Scrutiny III: RAISING OF LAZARUS (John 11:1–45)—Bound. Tied. Dead. Decayed. Evil that is bigger than personal choice, or even systems. Evil and sin unto death. Such death depletes and exhausts hope—what does it all mean? What is it all about? Why bother? Lazarus is dead. Such death forces everyone, in grief, to face their own death and the possible futility of life. Mary and Martha weep. And when the word arrives that Jesus is on the way, Martha runs to meet him feeling anger, fear, pain, frustration, seeking hope. "I am the resurrection and the life." Not for the end time only but for the now time. "Do you believe this? . . . Yes, Lord, I do believe." God's intervention is truly a restoration. The way of evil and death is not the way of the life-giving God. "Roll away the stone." Resistance, caution, comfort with the established. "Untie him and let him go free." They are sent to free Lazarus. We are sent to remove all that binds others, holding them prisoners of destruction. Death does not make a claim on Lazarus, on us. The victory over evil is conversion from hopelessness to hope, from meaninglessness to meaning, from corruption to life.*

• *What is it in your life, in your community, and in the world that is buried in the grip of death and needs the freedom of new life?*

_____

_____

_____

_____

_____

Celebrating the scrutinies:

The basic structure is the same for all three scrutinies. The scrutinies are celebrated after the homily. Usually the catechumens and candidates are dismissed from the assembly to continue their experience of the word. Then the elect are called forward, accompanied by their sponsors and godparents.

The presider invites the community to pray in silence for the elect. The elect are then invited to assume a posture of prayer—usually this is kneeling. Sponsors and godparents either kneel with them or stand by their side. In either case, the sponsors and godparents assure the elect through physical contact: hands on the shoulder or around the waist.

Prayers of intercession are prayed for the elect. These prayers are based on the needs of the elect, the community and the world. Usually they are sung by a cantor in a slow, deliberate and ascending movement. This is an extremely powerful moment in the ritual, and sponsors and godparents need to be by the side of the elect to assure support and acceptance.

Following the intercessions—and the deafening silence that ends the intercessions—the presider will pray a prayer of exorcism and freedom for the elect. Included in this prayer will be the laying on of hands on the elect. The sponsors and godparents are often invited to participate in this ritual gesture. If this is done, the sponsors and godparents would stand in front of the elect and silently place their hands on the head of the elect, praying for the continued freedom that only God can give.

The elect are then dismissed from the assembly to continue to break open their experience of the scrutiny and of the word proclaimed in the assembly. The sponsors and godparents join them after the dismissal of the faithful.

Penitential Rite for Candidates

Preparing for the penitential rite:

The adaptation of the Order of Christian Initiation of Adults distinguishes the ritual celebrations during Lent for the elect and the baptized but previously uncatechized adults. The elect, as mentioned above, celebrate the scrutinies. The already baptized celebrate a penitential rite, an adaptation of the scrutiny without the prayer of exorcism (cf. *RCIA,* n. 463). The intention of the penitential rite is the same as the scrutiny: to strengthen and purify the candidate.

The immediate preparation for the penitential rite will be provided by the initiation team. Sponsors will be an important part of that preparation, as was noted in the scrutiny preparation. The rite recommends one celebration of the penitential rite (Second Sunday of Lent, *RCIA,* n. 462). However, many parishes prefer to celebrate the penitential rite on the three scrutiny Sundays, making a clearer connection with the scrutiny experience of the elect.

> • *As with the scrutinies of the elect, the sponsor will need to spend time in prayer with the lectionary texts. If penitential rites are celebrated on the scrutiny Sundays (Third, Fourth, and/or Fifth Sundays of Lent), the sponsor can use the space provided above in the scrutiny section for personal reflection.*
> • *Lent II: Matthew 17:1–9. What are some of the fears/sins that keep you/your community from accepting the fullness of Christ and all that implies?*

_____

_____

_____

_____

_____

Celebrating the penitential rite:

The penitential rite is very similar to the scrutiny prayer described above. The major difference is the absence of the exorcism prayer. Sponsors can review the scrutiny celebration above for appropriate guidance for the celebration of the penitential rite. Some parishes choose to celebrate this penitential rite during a Word service rather than at the Sunday assembly of the eucharist. If that is the case, it is extremely important that the celebration happen in the midst of the community.

Presentations of Creed and the Lord's Prayer

Preparation for the presentations of the Creed and the Lord's Prayer:

The Order places the presentations of the Creed and the Lord's Prayer during the period of purification and enlightenment. However, a parish can elect to celebrate them during the period of the catechumenate.

As with the scrutinies, the formational preparation for the presentations is the task of the initiation team. During the months of praying the scriptures together and exploring the issues of Catholic Christian living, the essentials of the Creed and the life-style of disciples articulated in the Lord's Prayer will have been explored. As summary statements, the Creed and the Lord's Prayer are given to the elect and candidates who previously had not been catechized.

• *Prior to either celebration, the sponsor needs to spend time reflecting on his or her own understanding and appreciation of the Creed and Lord's Prayer as symbols of faith and prayerful living.*
• *Spend quality time reflecting on the meaning of the Creed. How is the Creed a summary statement for you of your faith?*

_____

_____

_____

_____

_____

• *Spend quality time reflecting on the meaning of the Lord's Prayer. How is the Lord's Prayer a summary statement for you of the posture of prayerful living?*

_____

_____

_____

_____

_____

Celebrating the presentations of the Creed and the Lord's Prayer:

The role of the sponsors and godparents during these presentations is fairly straightforward: they serve as witness and support. As witness, their presence at the presentations reminds the elect and candidates that these gifts of the community reflect the faith of the community. As support, the sponsors and godparents remind the elect and candidates that they will continue to be companions with them as they live the life of discipleship within this community.

The particulars of the presentations will vary from parish to parish. They are written rather simply, thus allowing room for adaptation and development. The particulars for these presentations will need to be discussed with the coordinator of initiation.

Specific information about purification and enlightenment in your parish community.

_____

_____

_____

_____

_____

Celebration of Sacraments of Initiation

The great feast of the Easter Vigil is the gathering of the Christian community to celebrate the Paschal Mystery: the death and resurrection of the Lord Jesus. It is at this time that the church celebrates the full sacramental initiation—baptism, confirmation, and eucharist—with those who have journeyed with the community in the catechumenate.

Immediate preparation for the celebration:

The preparation for the celebration of the sacraments of initiation at the Easter Vigil that sponsors and godparents need to be concerned about takes three different forms: the preparation rites on Holy Saturday, the preparations for the vigil itself, and the concrete needs of the elect and candidates.

The preparation rites on Holy Saturday begin the transition from the period of purification and enlightenment into the actual celebration of full sacramental initiation. The ritual text suggests that Holy Saturday be set aside as a day of prayer and reflection for the elect and candidates. This would be a good time to celebrate the preparation rites with the parish community, perhaps at Holy Saturday morning prayer. The rite gives options about the preparation rites that are to be celebrated: recitation of the Creed, ephpheta rite, and the choosing of a baptismal name. As with the intensifying rites of the period of the catechumenate, the presence of sponsors and godparents is primarily supportive during these rituals. The particulars of these celebrations will be provided by the coordinator of initiation.

The preparations for the vigil itself provide the sponsors, godparents, and the initiation team (including the presider) a wonderful opportunity to reflect critically together on the various movements of the Easter Vigil experience. Rather than simply rehearsing the ritual, all can explore the meaning of the water bath, the anointings, the prayers, and the like. Sponsors and godparents, of course, will need to take note of the particular instructions of the movement of the ritual to facilitate a good liturgical experience. Again, as with all the other rituals celebrated, the elect and candidates are not present for this, but rather are guided through the actual celebration by the sponsors, godparents and liturgical ministers.

Taking care of the concrete needs of the elect and candidates before the celebration is important. If the parish community is taking seriously the call to set Holy Saturday aside as a day of prayer and reflection for the elect and candidates, someone will need to tend to some of the details of life that need attention: baby sitting, picking up the dry cleaning, supper for the kids. While sponsors and godparents cannot necessarily assume all these roles, they can help the elect and candidates find appropriate people from the parish who can help, thus freeing them for a day of prayer and rest, free from those concerns.

Sponsors, as well as the rest of the faithful, can prepare to celebrate the great vigil by spending quality time with the lectionary texts and the primary symbols of the vigil.

Lectionary reflections:

While some parishes, unfortunately, have abandoned the practice of the extended liturgy of the word at the vigil, many more parishes are recognizing the value of the extended vigil and are creatively adapting it for their community. Whatever the practice might be in your community, spending time with all the texts provides a fuller context for the celebration.

a) Genesis 1:1–2:2. How have I experienced the goodness of God as creator in my life and in the world? How do I/we respond?

_____

_____

_____

b) Genesis 22:1–18. How is God present to me and the community in the midst of our sacrifices? How do I/we respond?

_____

_____

_____

c) Exodus 14:15–15:1. What is the path of salvation on which God is leading me and the community? How do I/we respond?

_____

_____

_____

d) Isaiah 54:5–14. How have I experienced the tenderness of God's love in my life and in the community? How do I/we respond?

_____

_____

_____

e) Isaiah 55:1–11. How do I experience God's faithfulness to me and to the community? How do I/we respond?

_____

_____

_____

f) Baruch 3:9–15, 34–4:4. What is the way of God that we are called to follow? How do I/we respond?

_____

_____

_____

g) Ezekiel 36:16–28. What does it mean to me and to this community that God has chosen us as God's people? How do I/we respond?

_____

_____

_____

h) Romans 6:3–11. What does it mean to me and to this community to be baptized into the death of Christ? How do I/we respond?

_____

_____

_____

i) Matthew 28:1–10 (Cycle A) or Mark 16:1–8 (Cycle B) or Luke 24:1–12 (Cycle C). How does the risen One make a claim on my life and the life of this community? How do I/we respond?

_____

_____

_____

Primary symbols reflection:

There are at least eight primary symbols that identify the Catholic Christian community, and all of them are part of the Easter Vigil. The primary symbols also include a gesture or movement as part of the symbol. Hence, it is not just bread, but the breaking and sharing of the bread. By recognizing the importance of the ritual gesture that accompanies the symbols, we avoid reducing symbols to things.

Please note that the following reflections are not to be used with the elect. They will be led into the experience of the symbols and then reflect on their meaning afterward. These reflections are for sponsors because they have already lived with these symbols in the community.

a) Assembly:

• *What are examples of the symbol of the assembly in my daily life?*

_____

_____

_____

• *Reflect on the scriptures that refer to the assembly. What does that teach me about the assembly?*

_____

_____

_____

_____

_____

• *What is the ritual gesture or movement that accompanies the symbol of the assembly?*

_____

_____

• *What does it mean to me and this community?*

_____

_____

_____

• *How does the symbol of the assembly draw me and the community into a deeper awareness of our call to live the mission of the reign of God?*

_____

_____

_____

b) Light/fire:

• *What are examples of light and fire in my daily life?*

_____

_____

_____

• *Reflect on the scriptures that refer to light/fire. What does that teach me about light/fire?*

_____

_____

_____

_____

_____

• *What is the ritual gesture or movement that accompanies the symbol of the light/fire?*

_____

_____

• *What does it mean to me and this community?*

_____

_____

_____

• *How does the symbol of light/fire draw me and the community into a deeper awareness of our call to live the mission of the reign of God?*

_____

_____

_____

c) Cross:

• *What are examples of crosses in my daily life?*

_____

_____

_____

• *Reflect on the scriptures that refer to the cross. What does that teach me about the cross?*

_____

_____

_____

_____

• *What is the ritual gesture or movement that accompanies the symbol of the cross?*

_____

_____

_____

• *What does it mean to me and this community?*

_____

_____

_____

• *How does the symbol of the cross draw me and the community into a deeper awareness of our call to live the mission of the reign of God?*

_____

_____

_____

d) Water:

• *What are examples of water in my daily life?*

_____

_____

_____

• *Reflect on the scriptures that refer to water. What does that teach me about water?*

_____

_____

_____

_____

_____

• *What is the ritual gesture or movement that accompanies the symbol of water?*

_____

_____

• *What does it mean to me and this community?*

_____

_____

_____

• *How does the symbol of water draw me and the community into a deeper awareness of our call to live the mission of the reign of God?*

_____

_____

_____

e) New Garment:

• *What are examples of the symbol of the new garment in my daily life?*

_____

_____

_____

• *Reflect on the scriptures that refer to new garments. What does that teach me about new garments?*

_____

_____

_____

_____

_____

• *What is the ritual gesture or movement that accompanies the symbol of the new garment?*

_____

_____

• *What does it mean to me and this community?*

_____

_____

_____

• *How does the symbol of the new garment draw me and the community into a deeper awareness of our call to live the mission of the reign of God?*

_____

_____

_____

f) Oil:

• *What are examples of oil in my daily life?*

_____

_____

_____

• *Reflect on the scriptures that refer to oil. What does that teach me about oil?*

_____

_____

_____

_____

• *What is the ritual gesture or movement that accompanies the symbol of oil?*

_____

_____

• *What does it mean to me and this community?*

_____

_____

_____

• *How does the symbol of oil draw me and the community into a deeper awareness of our call to live the mission of the reign of God?*

_____

_____

_____

g) Laying On of Hands:

• *What are examples of touch in my daily life?*

_____

_____

_____

• *Reflect on the scriptures that refer to touch/laying on of hands. What does that teach me about touch/laying on of hands?*

_____

_____

_____

_____

_____

• *What is the ritual gesture or movement that accompanies the symbol of touch (laying on of hands)?*

_____

_____

• *What does it mean to me and this community?*

_____

_____

_____

• *How does the symbol of touch (laying on of hands) draw me and the community into a deeper awareness of our call to live the mission of the reign of God?*

_____

_____

_____

b) Bread and Wine:

• *What are examples of bread and wine in my daily life?*

_____

_____

_____

• *Reflect on the scriptures that refer to bread and wine. What does that teach me about bread and wine?*

_____

_____

_____

_____

_____

• *What is the ritual gesture or movement that accompanies the symbol of bread and wine?*

_____

• *What does it mean to me and this community?*

_____

_____

_____

• *How does the symbol of bread and wine draw me and the community into a deeper awareness of our call to live the mission of the reign of God?*

_____

_____

_____

Celebrating the sacraments of initiation:

The liturgy of baptism follows the service of light and the liturgy of the word. Sponsors and godparents have been with the elect and candidates, participating in the prayer of the community. After the homily, the community prepares to celebrate the full sacramental initiation of the elect and candidates. The elect, accompanied by their sponsors and godparents, will be presented to the community. If the place of baptism is different from where the liturgy of the word was celebrated, the presider will invite the elect to process to the baptismal waters along with the sponsors, godparents and the rest of the community.

The community is invited to pray for the elect, followed by the proclamation of the litany of the saints. During this prayer, the elect are invited to either kneel or stand with heads bowed, supported throughout by the hands of sponsors and godparents reminding them they are not alone but in solidarity with this community. This is followed by the blessing of the water and the profession of faith of the elect.

The baptism follows immediately after the profession of faith. The elect, accompanied by their sponsors and godparents, are brought to the water bath for full-body immersion. Sponsors and godparents help the elect enter into the waters and witness the baptism. After the baptismal invocation and immersion in the name of the Trinity, the newly baptized emerge from the waters with the help of the sponsor and godparent. This is followed by the next baptism, until all have been baptized. Parishes that are not able to celebrate full-body immersion baptism will need to adjust the ritual to accommodate their particular needs.

Following the baptism, there is a series of rites that help expand and explain the meaning of the baptism experience: clothing with the new garment and the presentation of the candle. After the new garment has been given to the neophytes, the sponsors and godparents approach the Easter candle and light the candle they have been given to present to the neophytes.

At this point, many parishes send the neophytes with their sponsors and godparents to changing rooms. While this is happening, the community continues with its own renewal of baptismal promises, followed by the celebration of reception of the candidates into the full communion of the Catholic Church. The candidates, accompanied by their sponsors, come forward to publicly pronounce a profession of faith within the Catholic community.

The celebration of confirmation follows. The neophytes and the newly received, along with their sponsors and godparents, are instructed on the meaning of confirmation, followed by a period of prayer. The presider then extends hands over the neophytes and newly received, praying for the release of the Spirit in new ways in their lives. The sponsors and godparents place their hands on the shoulders of the neophytes and newly received.

The laying on of hands is followed by the anointing with chrism, the sealing of the sacrament. The celebration of confirmation marks the configuration of the baptized into the very person of the Christ. Thus, one is both claimed and commissioned for the servant life of the reign of God. Again, the sponsors and godparents accompany the neophytes and newly received and place their hands on their shoulders in support and affirmation.

After the celebration of confirmation, the neophytes and newly received now join the community of the faithful as they begin to celebrate the liturgy of the eucharist. For the first time, the neophytes and newly received participate in the prayers of the faithful and join in the prayer of the church at the table of the eucharist. They are reminded that it is to this table of the eucharist that they will come with all of the faithful to deepen their commitments as disciples—and it is from this table of the eucharist that they will be sent with all the faithful to continue the mission of Jesus, the Christ, in the world. The sponsors and godparents accompany the neophytes and newly received to share in the eucharist at the communion rite.

As with the other ritual experiences of the Order, it is important that sponsors and godparents spend time after the celebration of the Easter sacraments with the neophytes and newly received, reflecting on the experience and how the sacraments empower them. This is best done a few days after the experience when the power of the ritual is still fresh but has had time to seep into each person's life.

Specific information about the celebration of the initiation sacraments in your parish community:

_____

_____

_____

_____

_____

Period of Mystagogy

The primary place of mystagogical catechesis (i.e., the partaking and unfolding of the mysteries) is the Sunday eucharist during the Easter season, the Great Fifty Days. The newly initiated will continue to gather at the Sunday assembly, joined by their sponsors and godparents. However, now they will not be dismissed until the final dismissal of all the faithful at the end of mass. The homily during these weeks will help all the assembly focus on the important dimensions of unpacking the meaning of the initiation sacraments and discovering anew the call to be missioned as disciples.

An important dimension of the period of mystagogy is the witness offered by the neophytes to the community, as well as the public witness given by sponsors and godparents. The focus is on the experience of God that has been celebrated throughout the initiation process and how now they—neophytes, sponsors, godparents, members of the assembly—are called to be servants in new ways.

Many parishes complement the experience at the Sunday assembly with special gatherings for the newly initiated, sponsors and godparents to explore the meaning of the sacramental life and the demands of discipleship. This happens weekly until Pentecost, and then on a regular basis throughout the year. It is interesting to note that the Order of Christian Initiation of Adults has retrieved an ancient insight regarding sacramental preparation; namely, the church immerses one in the faith and symbols of the community, celebrates sacraments, and then begins to dialogue together on the meaning of the sacramental experience. Rather than telling people what sacraments are, the church leads inquirers into a sacramental experience. Then the more formal understanding of sacraments can be discussed (cf. National Statutes, n. 23). From all of that flows a clear vision of the life of discipleship—the sacraments empower us to be servants, to continue to participate in the mission of the reign of God in the world today. Sponsors and godparents participate in these gatherings.

Some dioceses invite all the newly initiated to celebrate the eucharist with the bishop. When this happens, sponsors and godparents also participate in this celebration.

By the time the period of mystagogy arrives, most sponsors, godparents, and newly initiated have developed relationships that endure beyond the initiation process. Reintegrated into the ordinary life of the parish community, they provide support to each other, continuing to share faith and prayer together.

Reflection on the Vigil Experience

The Easter Vigil is a powerful experience for everyone who celebrates it. In order for you, as sponsor, to help your neophyte experience and integrate the meaning of the Easter Vigil, you will need to spend time doing the same for yourself.

• *Recall your experience of the Easter Vigil.*
• *What were the dominant feelings during the vigil? Now?*

_____

_____

_____

_____

_____

• *What insights did you gain during the vigil? Now?*

_____

_____

_____

_____

_____

• *What did you learn from the vigil about discipleship?*

_____

_____

_____

• *About God?*

_____

_____

_____

• *About yourself?*

_____

_____

_____

• *About your neophyte?*

_____

_____

_____

• *About your parish community?*

_____

_____

_____

• *Return to your earlier reflection on the primary symbols of the Easter Vigil. How has your experience at the vigil expanded the meaning of each symbol?*
  a) Assembly:

_____

_____

_____

b) Light/fire:

_____

_____

_____

c) The cross:

_____

_____

_____

d) Water:

_____

_____

_____

e) New garment:

_____

_____

_____

f) Oil:

_____

_____

_____

g) Laying on of hands:

_____

_____

_____

h) Bread and wine:

_____

_____

_____

• *Collectively, what do these symbols demand of you with regard to your commitment as a disciple?*

_____

_____

_____

_____

_____

Easter Season Lectionary Reflection

The newly initiated, sponsors, godparents, and all the faithful will need to prepare the lectionary texts for the Sunday assembly. The period of mystagogy uses the lectionary readings from Cycle A (*RCIA,* n. 247).

Easter I: Acts 10:34, 37–43; Colossians 3:1–4 or 1 Corinthians 5:6–8; John 20:1–9.

_____

_____

_____

Easter II: Acts 4:42–47; 1 Peter 1:3–9; John 20:19–31.

_____

_____

_____

Easter III: Acts 2:14, 22–28; 1 Peter 1:17–21; Luke 24:13–35.

_____

_____

_____

Easter IV: Acts 2:14, 36–41; 1 Peter 2:20–25; John 10:1–10.

_____

_____

_____

Easter V: Acts 6:1–7; 1 Peter 2:4–9; John 14:1–12.

_____

_____

_____

Easter VI: Acts 8:5–8, 14–17; 1 Peter 3:15–18; John 14:15–21.

_____

_____

_____

Ascension: Acts 1:1–11; Ephesians 1:17–23; Matthew 28:16–20.

_____

_____

_____

Easter VII: Acts 1:12–14; 1 Peter 4:13–16; John 17:1–11.

_____

_____

_____

Pentecost vigil: Genesis 11:1–9 or Exodus 19:3–8, 16–20 or Ezekiel 37:1–14 or Joel 3:1–5; Romans 8:22–27; John 7:37–39.

_____

_____

_____

Pentecost: Acts 2:1–11; 1 Corinthians 12:3–7, 12–13; John 20:19–23.

_____

_____

_____

Specific information about mystagogy in your parish community:

_____

_____

_____

_____

_____

Part Two

Sponsor as Caring Companion

The ministry of sponsor is about getting to know another person and helping that person become part of our community of faith. Part One outlined the various expectations and roles of sponsoring within the context of the Order of Christian Initiation of Adults. Yet all of those responsibilities need to be rooted in a fundamental expectation: that the sponsor serves as a caring companion for the person seeking to celebrate the initiation commitment within the Catholic Christian community.

Serving as a caring companion means spending quality time with another person, answering questions, helping ask better questions, and sharing prayer and faith together. Such a relationship requires some basic levels of trust and acceptance, risk-taking through self-disclosure, the ability to truly listen to the other, and the ability to offer feedback and challenge to the other. In an understanding and non-judgmental relationship, one begins to feel the freedom to share significant parts of his or her life with another person who, in turn, offers this same gift to the other. This results in greater trust, understanding and acceptance. To serve as a caring companion is to walk on the journey of faith with another person because of one's personal conviction of the meaningfulness of the journey.

A key dimension of this relationship is caring. Caring for another person means: to be truly present to that person, to help that person to grow freely and achieve a deeper sense of self-congruence, to honestly affirm the story of another

109

and of oneself, and to foster a heightened sense of mystery. The experience of caring is one of acceptance (i.e., valuing the person as an individual of worth, regardless of external behaviors), understanding (i.e., trying to get into the experience of the other in order to try to see reality and the other's feelings about reality from his or her vantage point), and the effective communication of both (i.e., creating an atmosphere wherein the other can freely move into further self-exploration).

Serving as a caring companion and getting to know another person involve learnable skills and attitudes, many of which we use in an unreflective manner most of the time. Part Two will focus on some of the skills and attitudes that enhance the sponsoring relationship. Specifically, this section will focus on: being truly present to another through basic communication skills; helping another to grow freely by building trust in relationships and offering honest confrontation when necessary; affirming the story of another through insights on storytelling and self-disclosure; and fostering the sense of the mystery of another through prayer and faith-sharing.

Throughout this section of the workbook, sponsors will be encouraged to join with other sponsors in various activities and exercises. A word or two about these activities. First of all, you are the gate-keeper of your experience: you determine the level and content of your sharing in these activities. You do not have to share anything you do not want to share—this is not therapy. Second, all sharing should be guarded as confidential. None of us have the right to share someone else's story without their explicit permission. Third, you are invited to be open to the gift of the other person's sharing, welcoming and respecting it as someone's gift to you. Lastly, give yourself permission to enter into the experiences with an openness and receptivity to the insights you can gain from your companions, this resource, and your own reflection.

5

Presence: Being Truly Present to Another

Introduction

Essential to caring is the ability to listen to the other, to be truly present to that person. It is impossible to overemphasize the immense need people have to be truly listened to, to be taken seriously, and to be understood. The caring person is one who desires to discover who the other person is, entering into the relationship with a profound respect for the sacredness of the other. By truly listening, the caring person discovers the other by "getting into his or her skin" and seeing the world through his or her eyes, as well as being in tune with one's own feelings and perceptions.

Listening is a difficult task because it calls for a full investment from an individual. Many pretend to listen, when in reality they only hear words or sounds and are not present to the other person. In those situations, we convince ourselves that we are listening, but our own concerns and preoccupations are more important than what the other is saying. Our inattentiveness betrays our attitude.

Sponsoring Relationship

One of the most important dimensions of the sponsoring relationship is how sponsors communicate their care and support to the catechumens and candidates. While the important sharing of information about our community is a part of all of this, the genuine concern sponsors have for the catechumens and candidates needs to be expressed in a way that is both recognizable and convincing. Often what that means is that we need to reflect on how we are communicators in our daily lives, how we express our concern to others, and become more intentional about that in this particular relationship.

In this chapter, therefore, we will explore: basic communication skills, such as active listening, the use of body language, and feedback.

Exercise: Basic Communication

• *Join with another sponsor for this activity.*
• *Spend private time reflecting on how you would complete this sentence: "When I think about my future, I hope . . ."*

_____

_____

_____

_____

_____

• *When both of you have reflected on this, one of you begins to share your response that completes the statement. The second person listens.*
• *When the speaker is finished, the listener then restates what the speaker said using the listener's own words.*
• *If the listener conveys the best sense of the speaker's sharing, the speaker says so. Otherwise, the speaker clarifies the listener's response and the listener tries again until the speaker is satisfied that the best sense of his or her message has been returned by the listener.*
• *Then the roles are reversed and the previous listener now shares his or her reflections. The exercise continues as noted above until he or she is satisfied that the best sense of his or her message has been received and returned.*
• *How well did you listen to your companion?*

_____

_____

• *List some of the essentials you did in order to enter into a listening experience with your companion:*

_____

_____

_____

_____

_____

• *What were some of your difficulties in listening?*

_____

_____

_____

_____

_____

• *What else could you have done to enhance the listening experience?*

_____

_____

_____

_____

_____

• Did your companion listen to you? How do you know?

_____

_____

_____

_____

_____

Exercise: Some Qualities of an Effective Communicator

• Reflect on your experience in the above exercise or on a recent experience where you were involved in an important dialogue with another person.
• Place a check mark next to the qualities you practiced during this conversation.
• On the scale next to each quality, circle the level indicating the regularity with which you practice this skill.

Level scale: 1 = Always practice
2 = Often practice
3 = Moderately practice
4 = Rarely practice
5 = Never practice

_____	*Consciously quieted myself*	1 2 3 4 5
_____	*Consciously aware of my body needs*	1 2 3 4 5
_____	*Consciously aware of my own feelings*	1 2 3 4 5
_____	*Aware of body language of companion*	1 2 3 4 5
_____	*Did not rush my companion*	1 2 3 4 5
_____	*Treated companion as an adult*	1 2 3 4 5
_____	*Affirmed my companion*	1 2 3 4 5
_____	*Listened for the main ideas*	1 2 3 4 5

_____	*Withheld judgment*	1	2	3	4	5
_____	*Avoided telling companion how to feel*	1	2	3	4	5
_____	*Did not offer advice or solutions*	1	2	3	4	5
_____	*Freely asked for clarifications*	1	2	3	4	5
_____	*Used my body to express interest*	1	2	3	4	5
_____	*Expressed appropriate empathy*	1	2	3	4	5
_____	*Did not formulate response while companion was talking*	1	2	3	4	5
_____	*Did not finish sentences for companion*	1	2	3	4	5
_____	*Expressed myself with honesty*	1	2	3	4	5
_____	*Comfortable with the use of appropriate silence*	1	2	3	4	5
_____	*Able to restate what the companion shared*	1	2	3	4	5
_____	*Directly expressed my feelings*	1	2	3	4	5
_____	*Avoided assuming motives for actions but expressed what was observed*	1	2	3	4	5
_____	*Offered feedback without judging its value or worth*	1	2	3	4	5
_____	*Remained concrete and specific with my feedback*	1	2	3	4	5
_____	*Left responsibility to change with the other rather than pressuring*	1	2	3	4	5
_____	*Gave immediate feedback rather than postponing until later*	1	2	3	4	5

List other dimensions of the listening experience that you find helpful for effective communication:

_____ _____ 1 2 3 4 5

_____ _____ 1 2 3 4 5

_____ _____ 1 2 3 4 5

_____ _____ _ *1 2 3 4 5*

_____ _____ _ *1 2 3 4 5*

_____ _____ _ *1 2 3 4 5*

Helpful Guidelines for Effective Communication

The art of communication consists in creating a space within which persons can speak frankly, without feeling judged or solved. It is not casually hearing, but allowing the words—spoken and unspoken—to become part of you, challenging you, changing you. Communication in general, and listening in particular, is intentional and demands one's focused attention. It is not about solutions or quick assessments. It is wasting time with another person, allowing to emerge the insights that can only emerge slowly. All caring people already engage in some level of effective communication already. They have learned the skills by recognizing when they have been cared for by others, and imitated those skills. Becoming more effective communicators, therefore, is more a matter of recognizing and becoming more intentional about many things we already are doing in communication, as well as changing those things we do that inhibit openness in communication. In that sense, effective communication is a tutored activity. That is, we need to spend time and be formed into effective communicators.

Following are guidelines to assist us in the tutoring process. The goal is that one would be more intentional about these skills. However, the natural focus is on the person we are listening to and our response, rather than on the guidelines and skills noted below.

Appropriate Preparation

Most of us, when we are engaged in casual conversation, find ourselves distracted by either internal or external stimuli. Something the person says triggers another thought. Or perhaps we were already preoccupied when we encountered the person. Or perhaps something happens across the street that sets off a whole series of thoughts and wanderings. Whatever the circumstances, most of us recognize that casual conversation, however well-intentioned, does not always capture our full attention. Then something happens. Your neighbor says, "I need to talk with you."

Or a friend on the phone says, "Bonnie, I wish you were here so we could talk face-to-face." Suddenly we find ourselves saying (and doing) things like: "Wait a second. Let me put the kids in the playroom so I can really listen to you." Or, "Can I call you back in a minute because the tea kettle is whistling. Let me pour a cup of tea so I can sit and really listen." Or, "Why don't we go inside for a minute so we can talk and be away from those cars." Or, "Close my office door so we won't be disturbed." Instinctively, when we recognize someone's need or when they have sparked our interest, we want to "clear the decks" and be available to them.

Taking a clue from those experiences, it seems reasonable that when we enter into conversation that is more than casual, we need to prepare ourselves for the encounter so that we can be most available to the other person. Such preparation is usually very simple and very natural for most of us. Sometimes, however, we will need to be intentional and explicit about such preparation. While we will explore three dimensions of preparation, none of them really can be seen as distinct from the other; they are interrelated. For the sake of exploration, however, we will see them as three dimensions of preparation.

1) Consciously quieted myself:

Exercise: Chatter Conflict

• *Pair off with a companion. One person prepares to talk about something important that includes a great deal of details (perhaps reading facts from the newspaper). The other person begins to recite something silently to him or herself (such as memorized prayers or the Gettysburg Address). While this silent recitation is going on, the other companion begins to tell the story with all the details. Reverse roles.*
• *What happened? Could you listen to your companion? If you did listen, did you find yourself stopping the internal recitation?*

_____

_____

_____

_____

_____

In order to focus on the other person and truly enter into dialogue, one needs to settle the clutter—both inside and outside. The classic example of the husband (or wife) reading the morning paper while the spouse talks about important issues is illustrative for us here. While somewhat of a caricature, it does highlight the need to put aside the other preoccupations one has in order to be present to the companion. Sometimes it is simply taking a moment to turn off the TV, put down the newspaper, or stop washing the dishes. Or it is taking a deep breath and giving the internal distractions permission to just be for now, knowing that you can return to them later. Or it might mean saying to the other that you are unable to really listen to him or her because you are so preoccupied. While that might be disappointing, it is less frustrating than someone sharing important issues with you without you truly listening.

2) Consciously aware of my body needs:

Exercise: Body Conscious

A quick way to become more conscious of your body is to take your hands and rub them together for a few moments. Focus on the rubbing. Now that you are body conscious, quickly scan your body using your mind's eye—see your feet, legs, until you see your whole body. Be aware of what your body is feeling and tend to its needs. Return to rubbing your hands during conversation if you find yourself drifting.

Another dimension of preparation is being actively conscious of your body. This is a simple inventory of your body to be sure that you are comfortable (yet not so comfortable that you fall asleep!) while talking with your companion. Physical distress can be a major distraction from truly listening to someone else. Your head may be nodding agreement, but your mind is focused on that back pain or that headache. When your body signals your need for rest or assistance, it is more honest to let your companion know that—and it is healthier for you.

3) Consciously aware of my own feelings: A third dimension of preparation deals with your own feelings and affective state. So much blockage in communication is the direct result of unrecognized and unowned feelings. If when you stop by to see me I am in a terrible mood because of a situation at the office, those feelings will be the lens through which I encounter you unless I am able to acknowledge those feelings. This does not mean one needs to verbalize the feelings to the companion, although sometimes that is very appropriate. The key, though, is being present to my affective state so I can monitor how I receive and respond to the other. Such intentional monitoring of feelings is not as difficult as it may sound, unless one has chosen to consistently avoid taking an affective inventory. Once a person has a sense of their feelings, he or she does not need to be dictated by them. This does not mean the feelings dissipate. But they do not have to govern how a person is present to another. There will be some occasions, however, when it will be clear that one's affective state is too turbulent for one to be an effective companion. As with everything else, honest communication of that will allow both companions to have a context and understanding.

Exercise: Identifying Feelings

Many of us have grown up in a society that did not assist us in identifying and accepting the various feelings we experience. This is heightened by the tendency to evaluate or judge the feelings. Feelings, of themselves, are the natural responses of our affect to certain stimuli; they are neither good nor bad—they just are. The evaluation or judgment is on what we do in response to the feelings. For example, if I am angry because of something you said, the experience of anger is normal. If I choose to swallow the anger, or react by punching you in the face, then my expression of the anger is inappropriate. I could also choose other responses, such as letting you know that I feel angry and talk about it, or acknowledge my anger and ventilate it through exercise. The anger, of itself, is normal, natural, and healthy.

We run into a problem when we are unable to identify the feelings we experience. It then becomes even more difficult to acknowledge them, integrate them, and not be dictated by them. This blocks communication.

• Following is a listing of feelings. Recall a time when you felt the particular feeling. In the space provided, describe the feeling either with words or through images.

Anxious: _____

_____

_____

Arrogant: _____

_____

_____

Bored: _____

_____

_____

Curious: _____

_____

_____

Ecstatic: _____

_____

_____

Enraged: _____

_____

_____

Frightened: _____

_____

_____

Grief: _____

_____

_____

Guilt: _____

Happiness: _____

Hopeful: _____

Hurt: _____

Indifferent: _____

Joy: _____

Loneliness: _____

Miserable: _____

_____

_____

Regretful: _____

_____

_____

Relieved: _____

_____

_____

Sad: _____

_____

_____

Withdrawn: _____

_____

_____

Operative Assumptions

Most of us have the best intentions when entering into the sponsoring relationship, or any relationship for that matter. We want to care and respond to the other, letting him or her know that he or she is valuable and important. And then we find the other person somewhat distant or even put off. And we wonder why. One possible reason is rooted in the basic assumptions we operate out of with regard to the relationship. If we really want to know what we believe about someone or something, look at our actions. Our basic assumptions inform our actions.

Let's explore a few examples . . .

Maria, an Italian immigrant, is forceful in her work for human rights. Believing that all people have a right to equal housing, opportunities, and the like, she involves herself in a variety of community activities. The work always gets done, but often her colleagues find themselves put off by Maria, and she can't understand why. After much reflection, Maria begins to recognize that beneath much of her action is anger for the way she was treated when she came to this country, and a subtle but pervasive sense that those who suffer through discrimination are a bit better than others. Somehow that anger and arrogance seeps through her actions. Someone else, with different assumptions, might be more effective.

Charles is a sponsor for Elizabeth. Charles has been a member of St. Catherine's parish for a number of years and is excited about sharing his faith with Catherine. He calls Catherine often and invites her to many parish events. Yet it is often uncomfortable when Charles and Elizabeth are together. Concerned, Charles approaches the sponsor coordinator, Phyllis. After spending time together, Phyllis is able to help Charles recognize that some of his assumptions about the catechumenate might be in the way: getting Elizabeth into the church is paramount (membership instead of discipleship); Elizabeth needs to learn about being Catholic (information instead of formation); Charles is responsible for showing Elizabeth the Catholic way of life (child-directed rather than adult-directed). After being able to acknowledge these attitudes, Charles could change them into healthier ones. Now Elizabeth can experience Charles' concern in a new way.

Unfortunately, many people don't take the necessary time to explore and evaluate their basic assumptions about particular dimensions of life. Yet, such a process is crucial for authentic living and for change to happen. Similarly, it is very important in effective communication because we might be "doing all the right things," but for poorly informed reasons. The message that will be communicated will not be the care we wanted to convey, but the underlying messages.

Basic assumptions can be changed. But first they must be identified.

Exercise: Some Assumptions

• *Reflect on your current catechumen or candidate. Describe the relationship.*

_____

_____

• *List the most significant things you have done for and/or with your catechu-men or candidate in the last few weeks.*

_____

_____

_____

• *Review your list. What are some of your underlying assumptions that emerge from your list. That is, what do your actions say about what you think or believe about initiation and your catechumen or candidate.*

_____

_____

_____

_____

_____

1) Treated companion as an adult: Adults are self-directing, able to make their own choices, and live with the results and consequences of those choices. They recognize that life is complex and, therefore, requires responses that are often nuanced: things are usually not black and white, crystal clear. An adult, while sometimes unsettled by such complexity, is not rendered impotent in the face of it. Rather, the adult is capable of making a responsible decision. Adults can also live with mistakes and learn from them. Adults also recognize themselves as connected to the global family of humanity. Hence, the mature adult is able to delay gratification of personal needs in order to respond to others' authentic needs.

2) Withheld judgment: The old axiom "hate the sin but not the sinner" is another version of what we are talking about here. It is easy to judge the actions or responses of another, especially with regard to something we have a strong opinion about, such as moral norms. A basic assumption that we need to operate out of is the respect for each person as created person. We may not approve of a person's choices—or, conversely, we may overwhelmingly approve a person's choices—but our posture of welcome and acceptance sees the valuable person, our brother and sister. Withholding judgment does not mean we cannot articulate our concerns about a topic, or offer our perspective. It does mean, though, that we do not burden the other with our judgment of them because of these situations. It is a posture of true humility to realize that we don't know the heart and motives of a person's actions. We can call people to accountability, but that is different than placing a judgment on them.

3) Affirmed companion: Affirmation as a value stands in contrast to the culturally accepted postures of competition, acquisition, and self-sufficiency. True affirmation is based on the basic value and dignity of the other. Affirming another is a way of recognizing gifts and growth in the other. Essentially, it is a way of saying that the other is appreciated, recognized, and valuable. When one is preoccupied with doing better than others (competition), exerting superiority through more skills or possessions (acquisition), or keeping others at a distance (self-sufficiency), then one is incapable of offering genuine affirmation. At best, those attempts at affirmation are experienced as hollow and empty, or manipulative. Authentic affirmation is other-focused.

4) Comfortable with the use of appropriate silence: In the busy and hectic world we live in, silence seems almost like an intrusion. Yet it is in silence that lives are nourished and able to grow. Too often, in conversation, we find the silence deafening. We want to talk through it. We fear the other might be uncomfortable with the silence. We think we should have something to say to them. And so we fill up the silence with the sounds of our voice and never make room for the issues that are shared to take root in both of our imaginations. Silence can be a respectful response to something shared by someone. It helps the listener resist the temptation to fix the situation, and allows the speaker to resonate with the sound of his or her own words after they are spoken. The basic assumption here is that silence is a healing balm, a necessary part of any conversation. It does not have to be frightening but, rather, inviting.

Exercise: Assumption Review and Edit

• *Return to your list of assumptions from the beginning of this section. Place a check next to those assumptions you feel are appropriate. Place an X next to those assumptions you feel are inappropriate.*

• Share the list of appropriate assumptions with other sponsors, asking for their feedback. Make any necessary adjustment to the list based on your dialogue.
• Choose one of the assumptions that you deemed inappropriate.
• Name the assumption:

_____

• Why do you think this assumption is inappropriate?

_____

_____

_____

• What would be a more appropriate assumption to replace it?

_____

_____

_____

• What do you need to do (or learn, or understand, etc.) in order to shift from the inappropriate to an appropriate assumption?

_____

_____

_____

• Repeat with each inappropriate assumption on your list.

Active Listening

We hear a great many things. Sometimes we may even feel bombarded with the amount of sound that we hear. But hearing is different than actively listening.

Hearing is a passive experience. Sound comes to us—usually uninvited—and may or may not have an impact or effect on us. Active listening, on the other hand, is an intentional way of receiving sound. It is an essential dimension of effective communication. Active listening is focused listening. It demands the preparation and assumptions mentioned above. And it demands some skills of its own.

Exercise: Listening Remembrance

• *Recall a recent experience when you truly felt listened to by another. Describe why you felt your companion listened to you.*

_____

_____

_____

_____

_____

• *List qualities that demonstrate to you that someone is truly listening to you.*

_____

_____

_____

_____

_____

1) Did not rush my companion: The active listener is patient and waits. He or she does not have a preconceived notion of what will be shared, and so waits expectantly for the gift of another's words and insights. The active listener also realizes that how one says something is as important as the words used.

2) Listened for the main ideas: The active listener tries to focus on the whole message: verbal and non-verbal. With a discerning ear and eye, the listener gleans the main ideas that are being communicated, and tries to see if they are consistent with the full message. This activity of the listener is a style of interpretation. The listener listens on two levels: the actual words spoken (and accompanying body language), and the possible meaning of the message. The listener tries not to impose his or her own interpretation on the message, but tries to sort the material objectively so the key points emerge. It could be too easy to get distracted by the details and miss the message.

3) Freely asked for clarification: The listener is able to stop the speaker when he or she is confused about a particular point, or senses an incongruence in the story. At this point, the listener asks for clarification. This is different than making a judgment on what was said. For example: "Earlier, George, you mentioned how important it is for you to be a member of the church, but now I hear you saying that you don't like to talk about joining the church with family or friends. I'm a bit confused about that. How do both opinions stand side by side?" Sometimes the clarification is to clear up a confusion about some of the facts of the story. Asking questions of clarification signals to the speaker that you are listening and want to understand.

4) Did not formulate response while companion was talking: No one has the corner on the market on this one. It seems many people can identify with this scenario: Someone is talking with you about something important. For a number of reasons ranging from the most altruistic to the most self-centered, the listener experiences an inner dialogue going on as soon as the speaker presses the right button. The button might be different in each situation, but at some point the speaker says something that allows the listener to think he or she knows what the full story is, and begins to prepare his or her response. Sometimes the listener even practices the response silently while the speaker continues. Now the moment has arrived: the listener offers his or her response, expecting the speaker to be at least mildly impressed. And the reaction is less than gratifying. What went wrong? What went wrong was that, while the listener (or hearer) was formulating a response, he or she was missing out on other key pieces of the conversation. Thus the spontaneity that signals that the listener has taken in the whole conversation, chewed on it, and is able to offer a response is lost in favor of a neatly packed response that usually misses the mark.

5) Did not finish sentences for companion: A cousin to the above-mentioned obstacle to listening is finishing someone's sentences for them. Besides being irritating for the speaker, completing another's sentences gives the impression that the listener somehow knows the story even before it has been told. It is one thing to assist someone who is searching for the right word to describe an experience. It is another to presume such intimate knowledge of the experience for the other person to the degree that one even thinks he or she can articulate it for the other person. The true listener needs to develop the asceticism of waiting and patience, giving the speaker the room and time needed to articulate his or her thoughts and feelings.

Body Language

People remember more of the visual message given than the verbal message. This is even truer if the visual message—our body language—is inconsistent with the verbal message. As embodied persons, we cannot stand outside of our bodies, pretending they are not there. Even the most controlled person gives the message of being in control. Our bodies are symbols of the messages we wish to communicate, and often communicate those messages without our explicit permission. Telling someone "Everything is alright, there's nothing to worry about," while averting one's eyes, looking away, and rushing the statement communicates more alarm than calm. Thus, the effective communicator attempts to be consistent with his or her messages: verbal and non-verbal. That means he or she spends time becoming comfortable with his or her body. And that he or she is able to begin to read the signals of the bodies of all involved in the conversation, including one's own.

Exercise: Body Charades

• *Join with at least one other sponsor for this exercise.*
• *List at least five feelings or attitudes.*

_____

_____

_____

• *Pick one and, without using words or signals, use your body (facial expressions, body position, etc.) to reveal the feeling or attitude to your companion(s).*

• *When someone correctly guesses the feeling or attitude you are demonstrating, discuss what body features helped offer clues.*
• *Reverse roles and continue for all five feelings or attributes.*

1) Aware of body language of companion: The listener needs to be attentive to the speaker's non-verbal communication. One's face and body are extremely communicative, especially of the emotional aspects of the message. The listener can often glean tremendous insight about the person and the message by being available to the messages sent by the body. Sitting with arms tightly folded, with my body turned away from you is as important a signal to you as my verbal content. Integrate those insights with my verbal expressions and the listener can get a fuller picture. At the same time, one wants to be cautious not to overreact to body language. The insights in the next section on awareness of one's own body language are useful for beginning to understand the body language of another.

2) Aware of how my body language communicates: We often rely on words for communication, but our body language is often the most significant contributor for effective communication, especially our facial expression and eye contact. Secondarily, our body posture, the use of our hands, and the appropriate space or distance we create influence the dialogue. What our bodies say gives greater indication of our underlying attitudes than what our words say. Hopefully, there is a congruence between our body language and our verbal expression. Among other things, our bodies tell us how close we are prepared to be with the other(s), how relaxed we are, and how much interest we have in the other and what the other is saying.

Following are a few communicator signals we give with our bodies that would be helpful for an effective communicator to be aware of:

a) Facial expressions: Our facial expressions need to vary to express the feelings conveyed. The permanent smile suggests to another that something else is going on. Allow facial gestures to be natural. Notice similar incongruence when another is talking. For example, if someone is expressing their sense of hope and yet their face looks despairing, take note.

b) Eye contact: The eyes have often been called the windows of the soul. They disclose more than words could ever tell. An effective listener is comfortable using direct eye contact with another, using fairly long glances but not staring at the other. It is appropriate to look more while listening and less while talking. Hence, don't be concerned when the person you are speaking with turns his or her gaze away from you during the conversation. While that might be a signal of avoidance, it could also mean the person is doing some internal work to organize his or her ideas.

c) Voice: The quality of one's verbal expressions conveys more of a message than the words. Here we are referring to volume, tone, pitch and pace.

d) Posture: A more attentive posture is one that leans forward, turned toward the other, with arms open. A relaxed posture is one that leans back, with head up. A closed or tight posture is one when arms and/or legs are crossed, the person sits erect and stiff, and is not turned toward the other.

e) Touch: The level of comfortableness between persons determines the amount of touch that goes on in conversation. Care and support can be expressed by brief touches to acceptable areas of the other's body—e.g., shoulder or arm. Some touch can be more intrusive than welcoming: sudden, abrupt, or prolonged touches or touching more private parts of the body, e.g., face, person's hair.

f) Distance: We all have our personal space that we move in and out of at various levels with various people. Moving too close to someone may cause them to feel invaded. Respect the other's space.

g) Gesture: The use of one's hands can add to the meaning, help clarify, or emphasize a particular point. Broad gestures for personal conversation can be disruptive; abundant gestures can be distracting. Hand gestures can also indicate underlying concerns, such as clenched fists, or wrenching hands.

Responding to Another

An important part of the cycle of communication is being able to respond to another person after having had the chance to actively listen and allow oneself to be affected by the stories and feelings shared. Responding, though, is different from reacting. Reacting jumps into the conversation and alters it for whatever reason (it's too uncomfortable, she doesn't see things my way, I have a better idea) by directing the response of the speaker. Responding, on the other hand, respects the freedom of other persons and their ability to come to insight. Responding is how one communicates that he or she has received what was shared as valuable.

1) Avoided telling companion how to feel: We often do this innocently, but we catch ourselves saying things like: "Well, you must feel terrible" or "I would be so angry if I were you." In our attempts to affirm and support the other, we eclipse their freedom to recognize and own their own feelings. What can happen is that the other person can identify with your expression of feelings as a way of avoiding their

own feelings, or as a way of getting approval from you. Rather than telling someone how to feel in a certain situation, the good listener is able to reflect back with
the companion, giving appropriate space so that the companion can come to
personal insight.

2) Did not offer advice or solutions: Many of us say we want other people's
advice, until they give it to us. Then most of us find ourselves wondering why the
advice was offered, or feel compelled to follow the advice. Advice is best left to the
safety of the advice columns where it can have little impact on people's lived lives.
Giving advice sends the clear signal of a "take charge" attitude from the listener.
Perhaps sitting with another in his or her pain or joy is too much for the listener—
so he or she offers solutions or advice. The intention is to help. But in the long run,
advice only clouds the issues. When someone says to us, "Give me your advice on
this," they probably are asking you to help them sort out the issues, not provide the
solutions. On occasion, it is appropriate to offer advice when it emerges from the
wisdom of your lived experience. Under those circumstances, the advice (really, it
is a sharing of wisdom and not advice) is offered in a manner that suggests either
some possibilities or is given as a reflection on one's experience. It seems, however,
that the wise offer presence and wisdom, not advice and solutions.

3) Expressed appropriate empathy: Empathy is the ability to stand in the
shoes of the other person, to walk with the person in his or her situation without
taking on to oneself the feelings the person is experiencing. Empathy is not absorp-
tion or assimilation. It is the ability to be with the other without becoming the
other. For example, the listener is having a wonderful day. Life seems so full. The
companion stops by and is depressed because of situations at home: no one understands, no one will listen, she is afraid of what is happening in her relationship with
her spouse. The empathetic person is able to immerse him or herself in the pain of
the other, trying to know the pain (usually by remembering his or her own pain).
The empathetic person is able to express true care and concern, offering space for
the other, attending to his or her need. But the empathetic person does not suddenly become depressed because of the other's pain. While certain circumstances
may affect the listener deeply, absorbing or assimilating the other's feelings is not
healthy. Rather than being a companion, one becomes someone who is mired
down by the other. Empathy is being able to walk with the other and still keep one's
perspective. Of course, the opposite extreme would be to be detached from the
other's experience. Such a posture is as excluding as taking on the problems of
the other.

4) Expressed yourself with honesty: The true listener is able to express his or
her perceptions, reactions and feelings with honesty. There is no need to hide the

truth from the other. While there are some people who are apparently damaged by someone's honesty (especially when that honesty calls for some change), these individuals tend to be people who have very poorly defined egos and are very unstable psychologically. The majority of "mainline" people may find honesty uncomfortable or even painful, but are not destroyed by it. The listener, after assessing the situation (my reactions and feelings, your verbal and non-verbal messages), can respond to the other from that wisdom level. Saying things to impress ("I know exactly how you feel"), suggesting a quality of relationship that doesn't exist ("I feel so much closer to you now"), or disguising the truth so as not to offend ("I feel comfortable talking about that" with your arms and legs crossed, body turned away) in the long run erodes the relationship. This doesn't mean you steamroll the other person. One can patiently and carefully express oneself with honesty in a way that can be heard by the other person. In some situations, though, that might mean the frankness of a double-barrelled shotgun. Trust the relationship enough to be that honest if the circumstances warrant it.

5) **Able to restate what the companion shared:** The good listener is able to do more than simply repeat back to another what he or she has said. That is parroting. While that might help the companion to some degree, that is not communicating a message of presence or care.

Offering Feedback

As mentioned earlier, the ability to offer feedback to another person is an important part of the communication cycle. This is especially true in the sponsoring relationship because the catechumen will often share stories from his or her life, seeking the response of the sponsor.

1) **Directly expressed my feelings:** Being able to take ownership for feelings is also essential. No one causes our feelings. They may provide the stimuli that we are responding to, but other people do not cause our feelings. "You made me so mad," or "You make me so happy," are both inaccurate and obstacles for honest communication. Ownership of feelings is expressed in "I" statements: "I feel angry when I heard you say. . . ."; "I feel excited about spending the afternoon with you because. . . ." Talking about myself and owning my feelings invites another person to do the same.

Exercise: I Statements

Reflect on some recent feelings—we have them all the time—and complete the I statement below using your experience. Try using that basic structure of ex-

pressing owned feelings. "I feel (the feeling) when (situation/stimuli) because (your reasons)."

2) Avoided assuming motives for actions but expressed what was observed: However close we are to someone, we can at best only guess as to the reasons he or she does something. It is both presumptuous and alienating to ascribe certain motives to someone's actions. Even interpreting someone's actions can often be incorrect. Instead, clearly stating what you observe gives clear feedback to the other person. Instead of saying, "I can tell you are mad at me when you act that way," it would be more helpful to say something like, "You are red in the face and refuse to look at me while we are talking."

3) Offered feedback without judging its value or worth: Similar to assuming motives, this places your criteria or standards on the other person. Such evaluation places you in the role of a judge. This can also come out in statements such as, "You did what???"

4) Remained concrete and specific with my feedback: Generalities only breed confusion. Their use is a form of indirect feedback. "Sally, you are such a kind person," does not tell Sally what it is she has done that is perceived as kind. Focusing on the specific action or behavior helps an individual to understand your feelings, or make appropriate changes.

5) Left responsibility to change with the other rather than pressuring: If the other person is acting in a way that you think needs to change, or the other person hasn't caught on yet to following the life-style as you understand it, pressuring (however subtle) will not bring about true change. Truthful feedback is what you bring to another. What that person does with that information is his or her choice.

6) Gave immediate feedback rather than postponing until later: We lose the right to offer feedback, especially toxic feedback, the farther in time we are from the event. Clear and immediate feedback, even when it is difficult, keeps the lines of communication open and unobstructed.

Exercise: Developing Listening Skills

• *Review your responses to the opening exercise in light of the input on listening skills. You may want to change some of your responses at this time.*
• *Following is the same listing of qualities. Check the qualities that you identify as needing your focused attention. After the specific quality, write one concrete action that will assist you in developing the quality.*

• Return to the list on a regular basis to review and evaluate your development as a listener.

_____ *Consciously quieted myself:*

_____

_____

_____ *Consciously aware of my body needs:*

_____

_____

_____ *Consciously aware of my own feelings:*

_____

_____

_____ *Aware of body language of companion:*

_____

_____

_____ *Did not rush my companion:*

_____

_____

_____ *Treated companion as an adult:*

_____

_____

_____ *Affirmed my companion:*

_____

_____

_____ *Listened for the main ideas:*

_____

_____

_____ *Withheld judgment:*

_____

_____

_____ *Avoided telling companion how to feel:*

_____

_____

_____ *Did not offer advice or solutions:*

_____

_____

_____ *Freely asked for clarifications:*

_____

_____

_____ *Used my body to express interest:*

_____

_____

_____ *Expressed appropriate empathy:*

_____

_____

_____ *Did not formulate response while companion was talking:*

_____

_____

_____ *Did not finish sentences for companion:*

_____

_____

_____ *Expressed yourself with honesty:*

_____

_____

_____ *Comfortable with the use of appropriate silence:*

_____

_____

_____ *Able to restate what the companion shared:*

_____

_____

_____ _Directly expressed my feelings:_

_____

_____

_____ _Avoided assuming motives for actions but expressed what was observed:_

_____

_____

_____ _Offered feedback without judging its value or worth:_

_____

_____

_____ _Remained concrete and specific with my feedback:_

_____

_____

_____ _Left responsibility to change with the other rather than pressuring:_

_____

_____

_____ _Gave immediate feedback rather than postponing until later:_

_____

_____

6

Growth: Helping Another to Grow

Introduction

Being proficient in basic communication skills is not enough to foster a caring relationship. Another dimension of caring for another involves helping the other person to freely grow and achieve a deeper sense of self. Important components of these dimensions of caring include honesty, patience, and trust. As we respect and cherish the unique person the other is, we need to encourage his or her growth and development at his or her own rate and in response to his or her own needs. We cannot force growth or conversion in anyone anymore than we can force a tree to grow.

We must see the person as she or he truly is. We cannot hide behind masks that color or deceive our vision, if we are to be truly caring. Sometimes that is difficult —we may not like what we see because it challenges us too much, or because the person fails to meet our expectations, or demands too much. Honesty demands that we see the other person and ourselves as we truly are, not as we would like ourselves to be. Thus, honesty usually demands gentle confrontation when the facts seem to be in contradiction. The motivation for such confrontation is the growth of the individual and the community.

Encouraging the growth of another calls for patience if we are going to allow the growing process to take its own course. Patience does not mean simply sitting back and hoping against hope that the other will come around to a deeper awareness of self. Rather, patience calls for a giving of self, a participation in that act of becoming for the other. Patience is offering the gift of time to allow the other to discover self in one's own time. Within this element of patience, we discover the richness of waiting. This waiting helps communicate the message to another that he or she is worthwhile, that you are here for that person, a sense that it is okay. This waiting allows the other to experience the freedom of personal development without the unnecessary tension of achievement.

The ability to truly experience growth occurs in an atmosphere of trust. This is not an environment of overprotection, dominance, or subtle expressions of mistrust. Rather, it happens when one can let go of personal plans for the other, offering support for the individual's growth and development that demands risk and courage. In this environment, one can recognize and experience the power to grow to a level of responsibility for his or her own life.

Developing Trust in Relationships

It was clear from the beginning to June that she would not get along with her sponsor, Martha. Martha had been coming to the precatechumenate sessions faithfully, and always had something uplifting to say to the group, like "How wonderful it is that God is sending such beautiful people to our parish." Or "I have suffered a great deal in life but God has shown me how to live through it all and make the best of it." Whenever Martha shared these thoughts, June heard her own internal voice: "Lady, give me a break! Get real!" Imagine how surprised June was when Martha approached her that fateful night to let her know that she was her sponsor for the rest of the process.

It wasn't that Martha didn't try. No, June thought, Martha tried very hard. Too hard. Every week, at least once a week, Martha called June or even dropped by the house unexpectedly. She freely spoke of her experiences of God and often wanted to pray with June. June was amazed that anyone could be so public about God. June had already decided that she would never tell all that she felt about God; it was just too personal. And pray with Martha! How awkward! But June agreed every time if for no other reason but that it appeared to make Martha happy.

This had been going on for months now. June had become accustomed to Martha's ways and had even grown to wait for Martha's calls and visits. June found herself more vocal when she didn't agree with Martha, always careful not to hurt her. And soon she began to agree to go with Martha to some of the parish functions —and even to other events outside the parish. And she had to admit that Martha could usually weave a good story, leaving June feeling a bit warm inside. Yes, June thought Martha was a bit much, but had grown to like her. After awhile, Martha became as familiar as a good book or an old sweater.

June felt she kept Martha at a distance. She carefully chose what she shared with her and how much of her personal life she let Martha know about. June was even more private about her relationship with God. That's why June was so surprised that she felt she needed to talk with Martha tonight. The day had been very painful, unexpected. After the numbness of the shock of the day wore off, June found herself dialing Martha's number. "Please God, let her be home." Endless ringing. And then Martha's chipper voice: "Hello." "Martha, this is June. I need to talk with you. . . ."

The word *relationship* comes from the Latin *relatus,* to carry back. It is the experience of creating an environment in which there is a carrying back—a give and take. Relationship allows the possibility of returning to the other the gift received: a "carrying back" of myself. There are various levels or degrees of this. And sometimes we are involved in something other than a relationship: manipulation, passivity, coercion, denial. Relationship, on whatever level, demands a free back and forth.

Most relationships just don't happen. They develop and grow, requiring a lot of work and commitment. The sponsoring relationship is no different. Unlike other relationships that we freely choose, such as friends and lovers, the sponsoring relationship is usually one that is chosen for us.

Someone is a sponsor because he or she believes that one can experience the meaning of life within the context of the Christian experience of salvation and freedom. Furthermore, sponsors are willing to share that experience with others. However, this is not enough to create a relationship with the other. Sharing such important and personal experiences requires that a level of trust and care be developed in a relationship before such experiences can be heard, welcomed and shared. Serving as a sponsor means developing relationships based on trust.

Exercise: Creating a Trusting Environment

• Trust is a powerful bond created between two people. In sponsoring relationships, the sponsor takes the lead in the dialogue, offering an environment of care

within which the inquirer and catechumen feels it is safe to hear the message of God experienced in the life of this community and begin to respond to this good word.

• A good place to look to discover how to create an environment of trust is to look at our own experiences of trust and glean insights from them.

• Think about people you can say you trust. List their names:

_____

_____

• What are some of the qualities or characteristics of these people that caused you to think of them as people you trust?

_____

_____

_____

_____

• In light of these qualities or characteristics, what are the implications for the kinds of environments that you need to create as a sponsor to facilitate a basic level of trust? Be concrete and specific.

_____

_____

_____

_____

Keep those qualities and characteristics of trust in mind as you continue in this section of your workbook. To explore developing trust in relationships, we will need to look at the variety of relationships we experience and the place of the sponsoring relationship in that discussion.

Levels of Relationships

All of us have different types and levels of relationships, ranging from the most casual to the most intimate. How we relate and trust different people depends a great deal on the kind of relationship we have with them. For example, most of us presume that we can share very personal feelings and ideas with people who are very close to us, such as a spouse or best friend. Conversely, most of us find it at best awkward when someone we share a casual relationship with begins to reveal very intimate and personal things about him or herself. The variety or levels of relationships suggest levels of trust established that enable certain types or levels of self-disclosure.

Relationships, of their very nature, are unique because they involve unique individuals with unique circumstances. It is helpful, though, to provide some structure to understand levels of relationships, keeping in mind the artificial nature of such a discussion. As mentioned, relationships defy categorization and a seemingly casual relationship may, in fact, develop quickly into levels of intimate sharing. The structure proposed, hopefully, will allow us to see the varieties of our relationships in order to situate the sponsor relationship.

There are at least five levels of relationships most people are engaged in with others: the public level, the level of discussion of ideas, the level of dialogue, the level of the valuable, and the level of authentic intimacy. As the illustration below suggests, each of these levels of relationships is somehow related to the other, and usually presumes the previous levels of relationships are operative. Furthermore, relationships at a given level differ, and individuals may experience themselves moving in and out of levels with a particular person given a variety of circumstances. What is important for our discussion is that there are different levels of relationship that do exist.

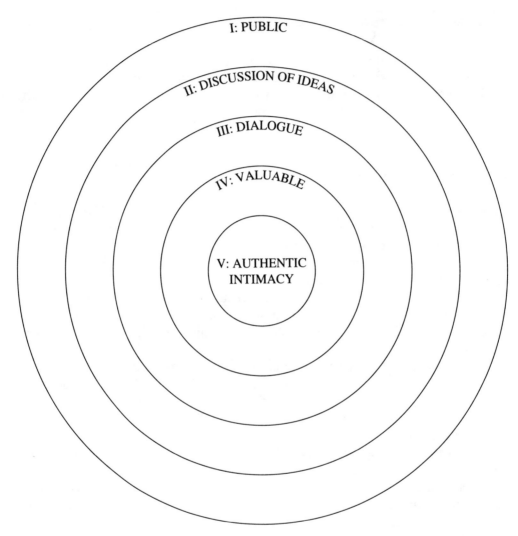

Figure 4

Level I—The public level: This is the level of relationship that we share with the general public. On this level, our conversations tend to be basic, general, and not very revealing of who we are. Our expectations of people in these relationships are minimal: adults treating other adults with dignity and respect. The people with whom we have these relationships are often people we may see regularly while we commute to work, colleagues in our office building we might meet on the elevator, or people who live in our housing complex whom we only meet at the mailbox or pass in the neighborhood.

• *Identify for yourself some people you share this level of relationship with:*

_____

_____

_____

• *How would you further expand the description of relationships at the public level?*

_____

_____

_____

Level II—The level of discussion of ideas: This is the level of relationship that we share with acquaintances and colleagues. On this level, our conversations tend to revolve around our ideas, issues, and concepts about work, life, religion, politics and the like. Although there is some level of self-disclosure, the conversation still stands outside of us, keeping the risks involved to a minimum—the exchange (and perhaps debate) over ideas. People learn about our ideas but not necessarily about ourselves. Our expectations of people in these relationships are greater than those in the previous level. We presume that they will listen to our ideas, respect us and our ideas, offer challenge in an adult manner, and not identify us with our ideas. The people with whom we have these relationships are often people we work with, commute with (such as car-pools), belong to discussion groups with, experience in a classroom environment, serve on a committee at work or at church with, or know as neighbors through a community group.

• *Identify for yourself some people you share this level of relationship with:*

_____

_____

_____

• How would you further expand the description of relationships at the level of ideas:

_____

_____

_____

Level III—The level of dialogue: This is the level of relationship that we share with some friends. On this level, our conversations tend to have a greater investment of ourselves. Not only do we express our ideas, but our feelings associated with the ideas. The potential for true dialogue—the active listening and sharing of insights—can happen because the other person is valued and respected for reasons other than simply being someone you know casually. There is a new level of openness and self-disclosure with people on this level of relationship. Often the conversations include issues of a more personal nature, such as home life or other relationships. The comfortability and ease of the relationship might also encourage people at this level to become engaged in a variety of activities together: social events, sports, visiting each other, running errands together, volunteering together. Our expectations of people in these relationships are much greater—we usually like being with them and talking with them and presume the feeling is shared. Other expectations might include: keeping in touch with each other—phone calls, letters, visits—even when there might be an absence of contact over a long period; involving the other in special events; and keeping the other informed of important changes in one's life, such as career changes or new romantic relationships. The people with whom we have these relationships are often people we seem to naturally gravitate toward in our varied settings: work, play, church, and social gatherings. Some of them we might call friends. Others we know simply as people we enjoy being with, enjoy sharing some of our lives with, but don't want to make large investments of time and energy with.

• Identify for yourself some people you share this level of relationship with:

_____

_____

_____

• How would you further expand the description of relationships at the level of dialogue:

_____

_____

_____

Level IV—The level of the valuable: This is the level of relationship that we share with good friends. On this level, our conversations and actions reflect what is truly valuable to us in our lives: we can express our ideas, our feelings, our hopes and dreams, and talk comfortably—to the extent anyone can talk comfortably—about things that are very important to us. Some of those things include: the quality of the relationship itself, one's relationship with God, one's concerns over certain responsibilities, and the like. Over the course of time and the natural testing of relationships, trust has been built that enables us to be frank, take risks, express care and concern, and involve the other in our life in meaningful ways. We spend time together, and look forward to continued time spent together in ways that are both enjoyable and affirming of our relationship. Furthermore, one feels the freedom to approach the other in one's need, confident that the other will be a source of support and care. People involved in these types of relationships have a sense that they are not alone in life, that there are people who care for them simply because they are, not because of what they can do or give to them. Our expectations of people in these relationships takes on a new focus. We feel we can be ourselves with them and they will accept us as we are, affirming our strengths and challenging us in our limitations. Not only do we spend time together working on projects, but we socialize together, help others in need, and keep in regular contact with each other. Usually there is a greater investment of time and energy in these relationships. Given our choices, we would want to spend our free time together. Sometimes a relationship on this level may develop the qualities of a romantic relation-ship, and the possibility of shared life together emerges. For the others, there continues to be the strengthening of the bonds of friendship based on shared values and experiences.

   • *Identify for yourself some people you share this level of relationship with:*

_____

_____

_____

   • *How would you further expand the description of relationships at the level of the valuable?*

_____

_____

_____

Level V—The level of authentic intimacy: This is the level of relationship that we probably share with very few, and sometimes are even afraid to share with ourselves. On this level, we struggle to allow the truth of who we are to emerge without the masks, the pretense. The various masks we wear (personas) are neces-sary for us to relate to so many people on so many levels. But this level of relation-ship occurs when we can be at home with ourselves and with another, and involves an intimacy that trusts even in the face of darkness that all will be well, and that the other loves and cares for me, and I love and care for the other. We recognize our need for each other not in the sense of co-dependency or clinging, for that is not authentic and healthy. We recognize that no one can give us an identity, yet our sense of self is deeply affected and enriched by the other. With this other, we can express our hopes, dreams, fears, joys. We can take risks that we would never dream of taking with other friends, colleagues, or acquaintances—we can let go and be with the other. The result of such vulnerability will include painful mo-ments of self-disclosure, of misunderstanding, of anger and hurt when fighting. But it will also include a sense of interdependence with another who truly loves and cares. Our expectations of people in these relationships seem simpler than in other relationships: trust has been forged and deepened, so that one simply expects the other to be the best self for the other, recognizing that in various seasons of one's life one will be that best self with varying levels of authenticity. But that one returns to such significant relationships for the support and affirmation needed to continue to discover the best self. These types of relationships tend to be few for most people; the intensity and depth of commitment they demand cannot be shared with many people. Such intimacy is the foundation for lasting significant relationships: marriage, "best friends," life partners. It is to this level of relationship and intimacy—authenticity and vulnerability—that God empowers and invites us for relationship with God and with ourselves.

• *Identify for yourself some people you share this level of relationship with:*

_____

_____

_____

• *How would you further expand the description of relationships at the level of authentic intimacy?*

_____

_____

_____

Level of relationship for sponsors: The levels of relationship outlined above are not exhaustive of all relationships, although they do give a general schema of relationships. However one identifies a relationship—acquaintance, colleague, friend, lover, spouse, guide, companion—we know there are various levels of commitment, expectations and trust involved in the relationship. It is fair to ask, then, what level of relationship is expected in the sponsoring relationship. This, of course, will differ in each relationship. Usually, given the expectations and responsibilities of sponsoring outlined in other parts of this book, and articulated through your parish initiation team, the sponsoring relationship seems to move between the levels of discussion/dialogue/valuable. Hopefully, we move beyond information sharing to some meaningful interaction and exchange that includes sharing our relationship with God. Furthermore, it seems unreasonable to expect that a sponsoring relationship would move to the level of authentic intimacy, or remain at the public level.

   • *Review the levels of relationship outlined above. What is the level of relationship you are/would be comfortable with for your sponsoring relationship? Why?*

   _____

   _____

   _____

   _____

   _____

   • *What are the expectations you have of the sponsoring relationship? Try to be as clear and concrete as possible:*

   _____

   _____

   _____

   _____

   _____

Developing Trust

One of the factors that helped distinguish the levels of relationships described above is the level of trust experienced in those relationships. Hopefully, it is clear by now that the sponsoring relationship is more than a casual one that requires the building of trust together in order for both people in the relationship to grow in their sharing with each other.

Earlier you listed qualities and characteristics of people you trusted. Review that list again and compare it to the behaviors and qualities involved in establishing trust that are listed below.

Ability to share personal events: Anyone can share ideas and facts. There is no real risk involved in that. However, when someone begins to share more personal events, such as feelings, how things are at home, how a relationship is doing, or some aspect of faith or prayer, then the listener gets the message that they can be trusted. This often opens the listener up to begin to share some of his or her life, and the relationship develops. Taking the lead—and taking the risk—begins to break down barriers and build trust.

Vulnerability: Someone who is vulnerable can express things as they are without needing to cover them up. Usually that leaves one open to attack. This is riskier if that which is shared is one's brokenness or woundedness. Yet when this is shared in freedom to another person, the receiver is graced with a heightened sense of trust. The message is clear: I believe you will not trample on me, not violate me, but will cherish and honor me and this information that I have shared with you. The ability to be vulnerable, and the level of vulnerability, will differ in each relationship. Sometimes it is imprudent to rush into such levels of self-disclosure quickly. But as with the reflections above on sharing, the more one opens his or her life story to another, the more that will be reciprocated. Taking the risk of revealing the truth of one's weakness and one's giftedness signals the building of trust.

Loyalty: We all know of fair-weather friends. They seem to be around for the feasting of life, but suddenly are hard to find when things get tough. And when the cause of our problems is ourselves—perhaps our doubts, depressions, addictions, anxieties, and the like—these supposed friends are long gone. But have no fear. They'll be back when trouble has passed. If we are a true student of life, however, we will know that these people are not people to be trusted. When we stand with another in their pain and misery, when we refuse to run away however frightening the circumstances, when we make it clear to another that whatever the shaming events that are going on does not mean he or she is shameful to us: then we send a clear message that we are committed to that person in good times and in bad times. Remaining loyal in the dark times of life lets another person know that you can be trusted.

Ability to accept the other: Some people are so irritating. And we seem to be free with our criticism and comments about every little thing they do that annoys us. And then we wonder why they avoid us. The message we send them is clear: You don't meet my expectations and standards. However, when we can see the individual in his or her uniqueness in a non-judgmental fashion, we are telling that person that he or she is worthwhile. Often our judgments of others come from our own unfinished agendas. It is a sign of maturity to see the other as other and not as a reflection or extension of ourselves or our issues. Such acceptance (which may not always include understanding of people's behaviors) helps the other to experience freedom and some level of vulnerability with us. Acceptance of the other is crucial for authentic trust to develop.

Ability to involve the other: When we are in mentoring type relationships, such as sponsoring, we can easily fall into the trap of believing that we have something to give to the other person that he or she does not have. Whatever that is—information, faith, God—we can begin to make decisions for us (sponsor and inquirer/catechumen) that are for our best interest because we already know where they should be at the end of it all. We know how often we should meet, when we should meet, where we should meet. We know the stuff that should be discussed and when he or she is ready to move on in the process. And usually the inquirer or catechumen willingly collaborates in our seduction. Our subtle message is: "You don't know what you want or need but I do, so trust me." But trust becomes the last thing established. Perhaps dependency forms, or admiration for our zealousness, but not trust. Trust incorporates the other in basic decisions that affect their lives, believing that they have something worthwhile and important to contribute to the process.

Expressing that you value the other: Another important dimension of building trust with another is being able to communicate how much we value others. We value them for themselves, but we also value their insights, dreams, visions, and hopes. We communicate this when we can share with them what is valuable to us (risky business sometimes), and invite them to share the valuable with us. In effect we are saying: "You are reverenced."

Being aware of the other's needs: Rarely, if ever, is life smooth. There are the ups and downs, the confusions and the clarity. This is especially true when we explore the journey of faith. Today we feel closer to God than ever before. And tomorrow we are confused and wishing we had never been part of this thing called the catechumenate. People who honestly care for us can pick up the signals of change in our lives and can communicate to us that they notice things are different and that it is okay. Additionally, they are sensitive to the issues and concerns in our lives and become advocates with us. We begin to trust these people because they are expressing to us that they have our well-being in mind. Such awareness is necessary for the building of trust.

Communicating: Mixed signals sent to another bring about confusion and the beginnings of suspicion. When we can't make sense of the messages we receive, whether verbal, written or through body language, or when they are inconsistent with another person's actions (you say you love me but you are always hurting me; you say you want to support me but you never ask what is happening in my life), then we become uncomfortable, less trusting. The words and the music just don't match. Keeping our communication clear and consistent builds trust and a sense of reliability.

General openness: A relationship that is going anywhere past casual conversation presumes that all the parties involved have something worthwhile to contribute and are willing to share it. Not everyone likes to do things the way we do. A clear signal to someone that trust is being established is our ability to explore a new experience together, especially if our companion is the one directing us in the experience. We are telling them that we believe he or she will not mislead us or hurt us. And that if things do get messed up, we know it was not intentional. Exploring new options engenders a feeling of trust.

Ability to be honest: At the heart of all of this is the ability to be honest, not to be deceitful. People know when we are handing them a line. This is more offensive when that line is coded in religious language to help create some aura of holiness or, conversely, false humility. While we might not be able to move to profound levels of self-disclosure and vulnerability with the people we sponsor, we can be honest with them. Sometimes that honesty means telling someone that this is as far as we can go in a particular sharing. Or expressing an uncomfortable feeling or insight or challenge. Or being willing to share our doubts and struggles rather than feeling compelled to provide the "right" answer. Or being able to say to a catechumen that it doesn't seem to be the right time to move on for whatever reasons. Such honesty doesn't mean a final decision is made. It means that a ground has been created on which we can explore the truth as we know it. It means we can be up front. Honesty says we can trust that tomorrow we will still be together because we don't have to lie to each other and then hide in embarrassment.

Exercise: Recognizing Self as Person of Trust

• *Most of us already show many of the qualities of trust in our personal relation-ships. The art of developing trust with someone is learning to translate the ways we naturally respond into concrete actions.*

• *Review the lists of behaviors and qualities for trust that you created at the beginning of the chapter, as well as the ones listed in the chapter. List the ones you experience yourself as comfortable with in your normal exchange with people, and give a concrete example of it in your life:*

_____

_____

_____

_____

_____

• *What qualities or behaviors do you need to spend time developing to enhance your relationships? List one concrete strategy to help you begin to incorporate that behavior:*

_____

_____

_____

_____

_____

7

Self-Disclosure: Affirming the Story of Oneself and Another

Introduction

People love to tell stories: stories of hope, pain, romance, struggle, victory, accomplishment. Stories are told in order to instruct, to pass on a tradition, to raise interest, to make a point, to heighten a moral sense, to tease the imagination. Stories can also be used to reveal oneself and to invite others to reveal themselves. In many ways, people are defined by the stories they tell, especially the stories they tell about themselves and what is valuable to them.

The Catholic Christian tradition is one of stories and storytelling. Over the years, those stories may have become codified and structured into precise theological language (doctrine and teaching) or into patterns of retelling the stories (ritual). Underneath all of that, however, are foundational and fundamental experiences of the gracious and gratuitous presence of God that brings healing and reconciliation to the everyday lives of people. Most clearly, for Christians, this is experienced in Jesus, the Christ. The ongoing manifestation of God's presence and grace continues to liberate and empower us as it has done throughout all of human history. Whenever that real presence is recognized, we are changed. And we tell the stories.

Before there are doctrines and teachings, there are the stories. The stories of individuals, such as the stories of Abraham and Sarah, Jonathan and David, Ruth and Naomi, David, Isaiah, and Esther; the stories of Mark, Mary, Thomas, John, the Magdalene, Andrew, Paul, Lydia, Penelope, Titus, and Priscilla; the stories of Cyril, Augustine, Thomas, Francis and Clare, Dominic, Teresa and John, and Ignatius; stories of Dorothy Day, Thomas Merton, Theresa of Calcutta, and John XXIII; and stories of Don, Maureen, Michael, Herman, Phyllis, David, Tony, Bonnie, and Joe. And the stories of communities, such as stories of the Hebrews and Luke's community in the past, and communities in South Africa, Cambodia and Ireland and in barrios and ghettos in the present. All of those stories are unified by the one story of God's marvelous deeds, the most marvelous in Jesus, the Christ. Such that, to this day, Christians still gather to remember the great stories—retelling them again and again and passing them on to the next generations—and to gather around the table of all stories to remember One who loved us by his death, restored life through his resurrection, and whom we celebrate as with us, calling us to be his story in the world.

Another dimension of affirming another's story is the art of questioning: not merely asking questions for more information, but helping another discover the art of questioning as a significant part of storytelling. As we shall see, authentic questions lead to new types of stories that can lead to more authentic choices.

The Sponsor as Storyteller

A third dimension of the caring relationship of sponsoring is the ability to affirm the story of oneself and another. The sponsor invites the catechumen or candidate to enter into the story of our community—the many and varied stories that make up that one story of faith—in order to be created with the identity of this community, to become part of our story. This storytelling takes on various dimensions: the central story of God in and through Jesus, the Christ, the ongoing story of the community of faith through history, the particular stories of this community of faith, the stories of the sponsor, and the stories of the catechumens and candidates.

Exercise: This Is Your Life

• *Consider your life as a great novel or play, filled with intrigue, romance, struggle, pain, and hope. Ultimately, though, your life story is a search for meaning.*

• *Look at the various seasons or movements of your life. Begin to list these seasons as if they were chapters of the book of your life.*

_____

_____

_____

_____

_____

• *Review the seasons or chapters of your life listed above. What line or phrase could summarize your life (to date) to serve as a title to your story?*

_____

_____

• *Consider one chapter of the chapters of your life. List the name of the chapter:*

_____

_____

• *Who were the significant people in your life at that time? List them and describe them, noting the influence and significance each had in your life.*

_____

_____

_____

_____

_____

_____

• *What were the significant events? Describe their impact on your life.*

_____

_____

_____

_____

_____

• *What are some of the stories of this period that mean something to you? List them—using words or phrases to help trigger your memory and imagination when you want to tell the story to another.*

_____

_____

_____

_____

_____

_____

• *What did your life during this season teach you about yourself? about other people? about life? about God?*

_____

_____

_____

_____

_____

_____

• *Continue with another chapter of your life.*

The Religious Dimension of Human Experience

One reason we tell stories is that they help us convey to another how we have come to encounter the mystery of life in its various forms and manifestations. Perhaps an encounter with creation or with another person or with our loneliness has brought us to a new awareness about ourselves or about life. While we could articulate a theory about all of that, the power to draw another into our experience comes from the stories we tell.

Another reason we tell stories is that they help us and others unpack the various levels of meaning in life. We discover in our storytelling that life is richer and more complex than our first perceptions may have led us to believe. Storytelling illuminates our experiences.

There are not two types of experiences (and hence, stories): secular and religious. Rather, there is one experience—human experience—and our interpretation of that experience. That interpretation can take various forms and can have various levels of meaning. One form or level of meaning can be a religious interpretation, i.e., discovering the dimensions of the experience (and hence, story) that opens us up to the awareness of God-with-us. This is especially true in those moments of our lives when we experience our limits, when we seem to be at wit's end.

Let's consider an example. Peter finds himself restless and dissatisfied with his job. He has spent many years developing a career, doing all the right things, and now at forty-six he feels like it is all for naught. He feels tempted to throw in the towel and just disappear. Being a responsible person, of course, he doesn't. But he finds himself fantasizing about various "options" to pull himself out of this funk: an affair, buying that sports car, or staying out late with the guys at the pool hall. Peter, with the help of friends, chooses to confront his loneliness and dis-ease. He comes to the realization that he is going through a mid-life transition and a period of reevaluation of his own priorities and values. With this interpretive lens, he begins to assess his needs and find healthy ways of attending to them.

Carl finds himself in the same situation. And, like Peter, he comes to a similar awareness. At the same time, Carl also recognizes that this reevaluation is an invitation for him to discover a new center of meaning in his life, and he looks to his religious tradition to help him in this quest. With the help of his community, Carl rediscovers the message of Jesus and the challenge of Jesus to his life-style.

Years later, when retelling the stories of their mid-life transitions, both men are able to talk about how they were confronted with their painful loneliness, the struggle not to give in to inappropriate responses, and how they found meaning in the experience. Peter's interpretation includes his commitment to become involved in volunteer work for humanitarian reasons. Carl's interpretation includes his commitment to embrace the mission of Jesus and become involved in service because of that mission. Similar experiences, similar responses. Carl's response, however, was a result of his dialogue with his faith tradition. In that experience, Carl was able to come to a new awareness of God's presence that invited him to a more authentic life-style. Carl was able to name a religious dimension of human experience.

Unfortunately, the public perception of religious experience (or more correctly, the religious dimension of human experience) is focused on extraordinary events: visions, locutions, marvelous and miraculous accounts of statues changing or paintings bleeding or the like. I would like to suggest that those extraordinary phenomena—whether real or not—do not have the power to change people's lives. The real power occurs when we are able to see the living and dynamic presence of God-with-us in our ordinary, daily experiences. The stories we then tell take on a religious significance because of our honest attempts to name God's presence in those events.

Exercise: Naming the Divine

• *Pair off with another sponsor for this exercise.*

• *Take a few moments and review your day. List some of the experiences of the day, when you were present and aware of life being lived (including painful moments). After each experience, list the feelings you felt (are feeling now) surrounding the experience. What was being said about life in that experience (don't use religious language)? about you? about God?*

_____

_____

_____

_____

_____

_____

• *Share with your companion—in story form—one or more of your experiences and your interpretation of the experiences.*

Telling the Stories

Perhaps it is clearer now that telling our stories of faith involves a basic sense of self-awareness of the stories of our own lives and God's weaving in our lives. This becomes more explicitly Christian when we relate those stories and our under-standing of God's weaving with the stories of the tradition: the great stories of Jesus, the Christ, along with the other stories of the Hebrew and Christian scriptures.

Part of the ministry of sponsoring is to help the catechumens and candidates begin to tell their stories and tease out an awareness of the divine in their stories. The ongoing process of evangelization is not to bring God, but to help awaken an awareness of God's presence that has been and is already present in their lives. However, in order to help someone share their story—and for you to affirm the presence of God in their story—the sponsor needs to share his or her own story.

Storytelling is different from giving a history of one's life. In fact, history-telling is a safe way of keeping everyone at a distance, including the teller. With history-telling, one does not really reveal oneself, thus remaining uninvolved and unchanged.

The style of history-telling may be familiar to most of us. A great deal of information is given—perhaps rattled off—with excessive detail and even personal reactions and feelings from the time of the event described. The burden of such detail, usually told in a somewhat detached and uninvolved manner by the teller, keeps the listener at bay. The history-teller holds the listener at arms length (at least!) and says, "Keep away."

History-telling is usually very accurate, almost like a detailed diary. The teller gives many facts and interpretations of the events recalled—perhaps even personal facts—but never gives the listener any access to the true inner life of the teller.

Rather than serving as an invitation to explore life with the teller, such history-telling creates a wall or barricade isolating listener from teller.

Such a style of personal disclosure—or really, lack of disclosure—is often overwhelming due to the excessive detail of facts. The experience is boring for the listener—and often for the teller—because the teller is disengaged from the information.

Storytelling is quite different from that. Storytelling paints a picture for the listener (and the teller) that is less concerned with the fine details and more concerned with revealing self. The storyteller knows that he or she will come to a new awareness of self in the very act of storytelling. That is the risk: that one becomes vulnerable enough to invite others into the process of self-realization that leads to self-revelation. Such storytelling doesn't fog the mind of the listener with excruciating and exact details, but excites and quickens the minds and hearts of all concerned, because the teller is invested, involved, standing naked and waiting for insight—from within and from the listener. The storyteller chooses carefully the pieces of the story to share because those pieces carry meaning and significance, even if the full impact is still unclear to the teller. Yet the teller knows that a part of him or herself is exposed for all to see when the story is told. And the storyteller experiences a new tension with the telling of the story: he or she wants to run and hide (such exposure!) and yet feels the pull to remain and relish the communal experience. Because storytelling moves one out of isolation into relationship, however minimal.

True storytelling serves as a bridge between people. Both sides—teller and listener—walk back and forth in dialogue. For stories, of their very nature, demand response from the listener (if he or she has listened) that can bring about insight. Stories break us open to each other, revealing new dimensions of ourselves. Storytelling is risk-taking.

Levels of Storytelling

There seems to be a natural progression or movement in storytelling. It is rare that one moves to a level of high self-disclosure with an acquaintance. Trust needs to be established. And yet, the freedom of storytelling is such that people do move to deeper and deeper levels with each other through the stories they tell.

Stories of Information: These are the stories, similar to the history-telling outlined above, that present basic facts without any personal investment nor personal interpretation. It is the most basic form of storytelling, presuming that a relationship will be built from this story. Otherwise, it is history-telling.

Stories of Meaningfulness: These are the rich stories that take the stories of information and weave them into tales of wonder! It is at this level that one begins to disclose more about oneself or one's community through the story. These stories are not rich in detail, but rich in images and affect. They help draw out the meaning of the story in the very telling of the story.

Stories of the Tradition: After weaving such marvelous tales of life and hope, of worry and pain, the storyteller and listener seek a new interpretive key to unpack the meaning of the story further. That is not to suggest that the meaning attributed to the story is invaluable. But part of the task of storytelling is to both expand and attach someone's story with larger stories. In our case, these larger stories are the stories of the Judeo-Christian community. And so we search the Tradition to find other stories that parallel our story. And as we remember the story of Jonathan and David, or Ruth and Naomi, then our story of love and friendship is expanded. Or when we remember the story of Jesus and the woman caught in adultery, our story of shame is healed.

The New Story: Expanded stories of friendship, healing stories of shame—stories bring about personal freedom. After allowing our stories to dialogue with the stories of the Tradition, we can reclaim our stories and allow them to evolve into new stories. We are part of Jonathan and David, or Jesus and the woman caught in adultery, and those stories are informed by our experience. A true sign of healing is when we can tell the stories without leaving out (or distorting) the painful parts.

Exercise: Telling Stories

• *Sit with another sponsor for this exercise. Together, you will tell stories about your lives, moving through the levels of storytelling outlined above.*
• *Choose a particular story that you want to share. Try to pick one that opens you up for further discovery.*
• *First begin with the facts of the story, the information. Perhaps you might want to jot down some of the details here.*

_____

_____

_____

_____

_____

• *When you are ready, begin to weave the story with images and feelings, expressing yourself and your experience. Feel free to offer your understanding and interpretation of your experience. Jot down any new insights you gained while telling this story.*

_____

_____

_____

_____

_____

• *Sit in silence together and mull over the story you have shared. Allow it to echo inside both of you. Then either you or your companion can begin to offer stories from the Tradition that either parallel or expand your story. Jot down some of those stories here.*

_____

_____

_____

_____

_____

• *Again, let those stories sink in and echo within you. When you are ready, share with your companion what hearing the stories of the tradition has done to you and your story. Jot your insights down.*

_____

_____

_____

_____

_____

• *Now allow your companion to tell his or her story, as outlined above. Jot down any insights you gained from listening to your companion's story.*

_____

_____

_____

_____

• *Jot down any new learnings you gained from the experience of storytelling.*

_____

_____

_____

_____

A People Who Ask

We are all full of questions. Questions of different styles, of different types. Questions are used to help communicate interest, or to express a lack of understanding. They also can be used to share a concern, or to help with self-reflection. Questions can also be abused when they are used to threaten, to confront, or to demonstrate superiority. Questions can facilitate communication or inhibit it.

Inasmuch as we are our story, we also are our questions. If we want to discover a sense of who we are and what is important in our lives, then we need to reflect on the kinds of questions we ask. Therefore, we need to not only be tellers of the stories, but hearers and listeners of the word in our midst.

The capacity to ask a question is distinctively human. We can stand back from our experience, reflect on it, become dissatisfied, desire "more," ask questions as to the meaning of it all. The foundational question, ultimately, is: "What's it all about?" Each question we ask, at whatever level, presumes some glimmer of knowledge or awareness already—we can't ask the question unless there is the desire to know more.

To help us understand this, let's look at our experience of loving. We humans are structured with a basic capacity to love: to desire love and to give love. When we meet someone to whom we are drawn, we find ourselves attracted, usually infatuated, until we "fall in love." Then we move into the throes of relationship with the other. Authentic love opens one up (a) to give away love, and (b) to recognize that this love relationship at this moment, however satisfying, is "not enough." This draws us into "more love" *ad infinitum.* We discover that we are structured toward infinite love. We also discover in the loving process that our basic longing and desire for true and authentic love can only be fulfilled by One that is infinite, the one we name God. That is not to say that the other "objects" of love are not important or need to be in competition with God. They, in fact, are revelatory of God's love. But they, alone, cannot satisfy. Augustine reminds us: "Our hearts are restless until they rest in you, O God."

The same is true of our questions. We begin by asking questions of information, which lead us to ask more questions that help move us to new levels of authentic humanity. As we move along, we don't ask only information questions, but begin to move to questions of meaning. These questions are complemented by new stories.

Levels of Questioning

Part of the human journey, then, is to invite ourselves and others into new levels of questioning. This presumes respect for the other, and a posture of hospitality that welcomes the other—with his or her questions—without judgement. The goal is not answers, but to help ask better questions. Questions help us move to new levels of awareness. And each one of us (and each community) needs to be asking different questions at different times of life. No question is poor unless it is not drawing one to a new level of awareness.

The life of discipleship is the movement—again and again—from questions of information to questions of transformation (which information will be part of). Many of us have become too pragmatic and practical regarding our faith, and need clear, concise answers, all wrapped up and ready to give away. This is not an encounter with Mystery. True faith is trust in relationship with God that is ever new, changing, dynamic. Human living is asking new and better questions so that the Mystery can be encountered, yet never fully grasped. This leads to new questions.

There seems to be a progression or development in the questioning process that leads us to new and deeper levels of insight and responsibility.

Questions of Fact: These questions are information questions that seek out concrete facts for understanding: who, what, when, where. These questions arise from a genuine (and hopefully, unbridled) curiosity. At this level of questioning, one wants clear answers as to what it means to be a disciple. But those answers ultimately do not satisfy.

Questions of Meaning and Truth: We become more inquisitive. We reflect on the original information and begin to wonder if it is true for me, what does it mean for me? How does it engage me? What does it bring to my life? This often satisfies for awhile. But, ultimately, one needs to address questions beneath even the meaning.

Questions of Value: What is authentic in all of this? What are the values, the operating assumptions in all of this? What is really important or of value in my life? Can I live these values for their sake as values? Even at the cost of my own life?

Questions of Responsible Love: How do I allow this to have an impact on my life? How am I changed? Where do I need to change? What am I choosing to do with my life because of all this? How is this flowing from my truest center?

Linking Stories with Questions

One of the ways we help people begin to ask life-questions for themselves is by the way we ask questions of them, and how we help them link their stories with new questions. Think back to the reflections on storytelling made earlier in this chapter. One of the ways we can help individuals move to new levels of self-revelation and

STORIES OF . . .	QUESTIONS OF . . .
	Fact
Information	
	Meaning, Truth
Meaningfulness	
	Value
Tradition	
	Responsible Love
My/Our New Story	

Figure 5

self-disclosure is by the style of questions we ask and the style of questions we help the inquirer ask.

Usually catechumens and candidates come with basic questions about facts. To stay at this level of inquiry is to mislead one into thinking that initiation concerns these facts rather than a way of life of the disciple. These questions of fact are responded to with basic stories of information. But then one is invited to ask new questions of meaning and truth, from which can flow stories of meaningfulness: how all of this is part of my life. This is where much of the dialogue ends for many people. But new questions of value arise now. What is underneath all of this? What are the operative values and assumptions? The response—the new stories— are the stories of our Tradition which bring to light basic values of the followers of Jesus. Then one is confronted with a new set of questions: can and will I embrace these demands of responsible love? The stories that emerge from such questions are the stories of the living Tradition: how you and I make fresh and new the scriptures by our lives of transforming love.

Creating an Environment for Storytelling and Questions

How does this happen? It happens when an environment has been created that welcomes the stories and questions and concerns of inquirers. Within this environment, it is important to honestly communicate at least the following:

HOSPITALITY: We welcome the stranger so that there will no longer be any stranger. One is made to feel truly welcome. This is different from instant intimacy. This is also different from a "coffee and doughnuts" hospitality. It is the hospitality marked and defined by the One who washes the feet of others in their need.

RESPECT: We value the other as the manifestation of God's presence, welcoming God's word to us in the other. We make clear to the other that he or she is worthy of our time and focus, without judgment or condemnation.

EMPATHY: We attempt to stand with the other in their experience, struggling to view their concerns from their perspective, trying to enter their world and become at home in it. This means acknowledging our own interpretative key to life and, as much as possible, putting it aside to hear with the ears of the other. This is different than assuming the identity or needs of the other.

GENUINENESS: All of this is done out of a sincere desire to care for and support, to help share what is important to you. While there is some level of skill in all of this, you are as honest with yourself (and with the other) as you can be throughout.

All of this is demonstrated by the verbal interactions we have, as well as by the posture and gesture of our bodies. Self-disclosure and self-exploration don't just happen. The catechumen or candidate needs to see the value and meaningfulness of moving with us to these levels of reflection. Creating an honest environment helps facilitate that. It is also important to note that these qualities—hospitality and the like—need to be perceived by the other in order for all of this to be effective. In other words, it must be real, and experienced.

8

Mystery: Fostering a Heightened Sense of Mystery

Introduction

The previous chapters have placed the focus on the healthy development of relationships and what that entails. All of that, however important, still does not get at the core of the sponsoring relationship. At the heart of this relationship is the desire to accompany another in the journey of faith, to acknowledge the presence of God in the life of the other and in the community, to walk together in the presence of Mystery. The communication and relational skills discussed so far gain their power and perspective within this context: openness to the Mystery of God.

Exercise: Personal Reflection

• *What does it mean to be open to the Mystery of God?*

_____

_____

_____

_____

_____

• *What do I understand to be God's will?*

_____

_____

_____

_____

_____

Mystery of God

When we refer to the Mystery of God, we do not mean mystery in the sense used by Agatha Christie and other mystery writers: something that needs to be solved. Nor is it meant to describe that large amount of material we cannot make sense of—hence, it all remains a mystery! The Mystery of God refers to the realization that there is an immediacy and intimacy to the experience of God (i.e., God is at the very center of our existence) and yet an otherness to that experience (i.e., God is beyond our full grasp and definitions). Another way of saying this is that Mystery is the experience of God that helps define us (i.e., gives us an identity as loved) and calls us into servanthood while at the same time it leaves us speechless, recognizing our creaturehood. The more one encounters the Mystery of God, the more one is drawn into it, yet can never exhaust it. Mystery is not something to be solved, but rather the experience of God to be lived. We can never fully apprehend it; yet we are always apprehended by the experience of God.

Thus, living in relationship to Mystery is living a full and abundant life in relationship with God, self and others. Such relationships inform and dictate the quality of our lives. Living life with abundance is a call to authentic living, of living for the other in self-sacrificing love. Such authentic living suggests that we become attentive to the signs and signals of life and love around us, that we begin to see the varied gifts of creation for what they are: avenues for awakening within us—individually and communally—the recognition of the divine. In this attentive posture that is open to things as they are and what they can become, we begin to search out the truth. We slowly unmask the deceptions and illusions to see the naked truth that challenges us, that invites us, that confronts us.

Living in the truth demands the disciplines of inquiry, of listening, of discernment. Having recognized the really true, we then must ask: Can I live this truth as a value? Can I live in such a way that the valuable is primary? In effect, we are asking if we can live for the other. When we can say yes to this, we choose responsible living that is consistent with the choices we have made, the values we have embraced. It is only in this responsible living that the true and authentic love modeled in Christ can emerge: living for the other in self-sacrificing love.

Such love is not the neediness of dysfunctional relationships, nor the inordinate service to others rooted in self-abasement and self-denial. Instead, it is a celebration of the individual and the individual's gifts in response to other people that recognizes the authentic well-being of the other—values espoused and lived by the Christ—and is paramount when rooted in justice and compassion. Thus, when one embraces a life-style that is rooted in true values, one risks one's very self for the other. In theological language, we call this embracing the demands of the reign of God. It was such a call to authentic living that was the hallmark of the life of Jesus of Nazareth, and it was for this that he was murdered.

Thus, abundant life in response to Mystery, is not a life cluttered with things and people. Rather, it is living in the trust and power that God's Spirit will strengthen us to embrace the demands of living values for the sake of values, whatever the cost. Abundant life means that we struggle for justice and freedom, compassion and laughter, hope and intimacy—for ourselves and all persons in our world now. It is a life-style that is contrary to the one often described in our culture: possessiveness, accumulation, power, distinction. But it is also a life-style that makes demands, causes suffering, and presents the possibility of death.

And all of this is cause for rejoicing. Not because of some morbid death-wish or a somber view of the world, but because the possibility of living our true selves is a free option for all of us. And when we take the risk and become attentive, search for the real and true, make judgments that reflect this, embrace values for the sake of values, and commit ourselves to these in responsible living, the result is healthier and more integrated life-styles that empower and free us and others. Another way of describing this is the discerning of God's will. Fundamentally, God's will is the well-being of all persons. It is not a stagnant blueprint of predesigned plans that God has drawn up, or a chess board on which we are moved, like pawns. God's will has everything to do with embracing the charisms given to us by God for a fuller and more authentic life. This discernment is relational and dynamic. It is living in the Mystery of God.

Living in the Mystery of God informs and directs Christian discipleship. It is the journey of raising up, examining, exploring, asking, becoming rooted in the values of the Jesus tradition so that our very humanity, that is so intimately linked with the humanity of every person, is embraced again and again. Our true heart's desire is to be in union with God, and that includes the rest of the human community. We can't do this alone; we are not so constructed. Even the contemplative is rooted in the human community.

Therefore, the place to begin (again and again) in discerning the presence of the Mystery of God is true self-knowledge: Who am I? What is important? What kind of life am I really living? What does my life and life-style say about what is valuable? Augustine reminds us: "You [God] were right before me but I could not find you; I could not find myself, how much less you." We discover in this a reminder of an important dimension of the spiritual life: God is closer to us and knows us better than we know our very selves. In discovering our true selves, we come to a deeper realization of God's presence. Such discovery demands our commitment to others as brothers and sisters. We never come to the fullness of abundant life without God and the rest of the human community.

Exercise: Discovering God with Us

• *Spend some quality time alone, reflecting on how you perceive and understand yourself.*
• *Who am I? How do I define myself?*

_____

_____

_____

_____

• *What are the gifts (charisms) given to me?*

_____

_____

_____

_____

_____

• *What is important in my life? (Clue: where do you spend your time and energy?)*

_____

_____

_____

_____

_____

• *What kind of life am I really living?*

_____

_____

_____

_____

_____

• *What do my life and life-style say about what is valuable?*

_____

_____

_____

_____

_____

• *How do I think God describes me?*

_____

_____

_____

_____

_____

• *As I reflect on the patterns of my life, what do I recognize as God's call to me?*

_____

_____

_____

_____

_____

• *What do I need in my life now to be more faithful to God's call?*

_____

_____

_____

_____

_____

The Mystery of the Other

All of this becomes more critical in the sponsor relationship. If we perceive that our role is to "get the person in" to the church, or help "solve their problems," we will spend more time trying to create the other into our vision of living the Catholic Christian life, rather than truly listening and respecting the deep sacredness of the individual person, i.e., the mystery of the other. The caring person is one who is intimately aware of the great awe and mystery that is present in each human person. No two people are alike, and therefore, each person must be approached gently, with a profound respect for that person's life.

Exercise: Discovering God with Us in the Other

• *Spend some quality time alone, reflecting on your relationship with your catechumen or candidate.*
• *Visualize your catechumen or candidate. Be aware, not only of how she or he looks, but how you feel when remembering him or her.*
• *How do you describe this person?*

_____

_____

_____

_____

_____

• *What has he or she brought to your life?*

_____

_____

_____

_____

_____

• *What are the gifts (charisms) he or she brings to the community?*

_____

_____

_____

_____

• *What does he or she teach you?*

_____

_____

_____

_____

_____

• *How does God describe this person?*

_____

_____

_____

_____

_____

• *What do you know about God because of this person?*

_____

_____

_____

_____

_____

• *Spend time with your catechumen or candidate and share the fruit of your prayerful reflection.*

Christian Prayer

How do we stand in this kind of relationship of mystery—with ourselves, with our catechumen or candidate, with God? There are various ways of coming to recognize the Mystery of God in another, many of which have been mentioned earlier in this workbook. A particular manner of coming to this heightened awareness of the Mystery of God is in the posture and practice we name as Christian prayer. Here, in a specific way, sponsors can accompany catechumens and candidates as they explore (in fact, as we all continue to explore) God's call to continuing conversion and discipleship.

Exercise: Prayer Reflection

• *What is prayer?*

_____

_____

_____

_____

_____

• *When do you pray (how often, what time of day)?*

_____

_____

_____

_____

_____

• *Describe your style or manner of prayer (how do you pray)?*

_____

_____

_____

_____

Praying with Another

Fundamentally, prayer is about one's relationship with God and with one's self in the midst of the community. Therefore, prayer is very relational.

How and when one prays says more about what one really believes about prayer than one's definition of prayer. Look at your personal experience of prayer and compare it with your definition of prayer. Are they related or does your practice of prayer suggest a different definition of prayer than the one you gave?

> • *Take a moment and write out a new definition of prayer based on your experience of prayer.*

_____

_____

_____

_____

_____

Some Theological Foundations for Prayer

Now let's look at some foundational assumptions for a theology of prayer that can affirm and expand our own notions of prayer. After each assumption, there will be space for you to write how this dimension is a part of your prayer, or how you are challenged to bring this dimension into your prayer.

1. God's love is the starting point. God allures, leads, draws us. We do not summon God's presence but, in fact, are summoned and beckoned by God's very presence to respond in some way, and prayer becomes one form of that response.

> • *How conscious are you of God's loving presence that calls you to prayer?*

_____

2. Prayer is about relationship with God. It changes as the relationship changes as well as when one's images that construct the relationship change (i.e.,

images of God, self, community, church, to name a few). For example, during one season of your life your sense of God is one of benevolent parent. At a later season, your image of God is one of friend or spouse.

• *Is your prayer reflective of your relationship with God?*

_____

• *What is your image of God?*

_____

_____

_____

_____

3. Prayer is an intentional activity and way of life. It is more than responding to internal images, impulses, drives, urges and the like. They are helpful to the prayer process, but prayer expands us beyond the images.

• *Do you balance your moments of spontaneous prayer throughout the day with chosen, intentional moments of prayer?*

_____

4. There is no right way to pray because prayer is unique to each person and to each community. However, there are "wrong" ways to pray in the Christian tradition: magic, manipulation, coercion, to name a few.

• *Is your focus of prayer on relationship with God or on what you can get out of this?*

_____

5. Christian prayer is always trinitarian in its focus: the experience of the death-resurrection of Christ, through the power of the Spirit, in the name of the creator God.

• *What is the normative focus of your prayer?*

_____

6. Prayer is about the life of conversion and discipleship. If the experience of prayer leaves us unchanged or more focused on self, then we need to question whether that was indeed prayer. Prayer thrusts us into the mission of the reign of God, thrusts us into service for the world community to proclaim the new day of God's presence.

• *How does your prayer empower you in charity and justice?*

_____

_____

_____

7. Prayer is both private and communal. In communal terms, it is also liturgical in the Roman Catholic tradition. Therefore, there needs to be a healthy integration and balance between private and communal-liturgical prayer.

• *Is your experience of communal and liturgical prayer still focused on private and personal needs?*

_____

How You Learned to Pray: Gleaning Insights

Now, let's put some flesh on these foundational assumptions for prayer by exploring again your experience of prayer. And from that, hopefully, you will be able to tease out some guidelines for helping others to pray.

• *What are your earliest recollections of prayer?*

_____

_____

_____

_____

_____

• *Who taught you to pray?*

_____

_____

What our concern needs to be is not the kinds of prayer that we are engaged in, but the environment of prayer that we create that helps the new member of the community, who is seeking to understand God's will, come to know something of God within the context of the Roman Catholic experience.

• *Based on your reflections on prayer, list some of the positive and healthy "qualities" or "characteristics" of those initial experiences of prayer.*

_____

_____

_____

_____

_____

Sharing Prayer with Another: Some Elements

What you have just done is list basic elements for sharing prayer with another person. Our best teachers for this are those who taught us how to pray. And how did most of them do that? By praying with us, by mentoring us in prayer through example. That is key for praying with others. We teach others how to pray by praying with them. We encourage a healthy sense of prayer by making sure that our prayer is built on sound theological principles.

> • *Review your list of characteristics, and mark those which are rooted in a sound theology of prayer (you might want to return to the theological assumptions listed earlier).*
> • *Place question marks next to those that leave you wondering if they reflect a healthy vision of prayer. Discuss those with other sponsors or your sponsor coordinator.*

Hopefully, as a way of summarizing your experience of prayer and your listing of characteristics, the following elements for prayer in the Roman Catholic tradition can help you in leading others in prayer.

1. Development of a symbolic consciousness. This means that we slowly begin to expose those coming to the community to the primary symbols of the community: word, water, fire, salt, bread and wine, oil, touch, white garment, and assembled people (the Easter Vigil is the context for understanding these symbols). They will then begin to see the simplicity of symbols used in prayer. Part of the "Catholic Difference" is our fundamental belief in the power of the incarnation, and hence, our sacramental view of the world: that God's revelation and presence is mediated through creation.

> • *How can you help highlight the symbolic dimension of Christian living and prayer?*

_____

_____

_____

_____

_____

2. The formal experiences of prayer need to be both personal and communal. The prayer experiences need to be structured so that individuals have time for their own personal expression of prayer (and that does not necessarily have to be vocal-

ized) and the important (and essential) dimension of communal prayer begins to be established. For example, it might mean reciting together a psalm, or beginning to learn together some of the traditional prayers of the community. Caution: Avoid using the Lord's Prayer because of its formative role in the whole process. This summary prayer of the disciple is ritually celebrated later in the catechumenate process when the catechumen has shown sufficient maturity to embrace the demands of that style of prayer.

• *During structured prayer times with your catechumen or candidate, how can you highlight this balance between individual and communal prayer?*

_____

_____

_____

_____

3. The prayer is to be based on scripture. The catechumen or candidate early on begins to see the great book of the stories of our community as a source of reflection and prayer. Perhaps a scripture story could be shared during prayer time or the reading of a psalm or text could be done together. The texts need to be approached with reverence and care.

• *How do you highlight the central role of scripture in prayer with your catechumen or candidate?*

_____

_____

_____

_____

4. The prayer should include the needs of others and how we are called in service of others. Initially, this might simply be through prayers of petition. But throughout the process, we need to be reminded again and again that we pray not only to enter into communion with God, but also to enter into communion and solidarity with our sisters and brothers throughout the world.

• How do you help highlight the importance of the needs of others in prayer with your catechumen or candidate?

_____

_____

_____

_____

_____

• List some other ideas you have about prayer with your catechumen or candidate.

_____

_____

_____

_____

_____

Final Reflection

• Review your earlier reflections on the Mystery of God, prayer and your experiences of prayer.

• *How has this reflection on the Mystery of God and prayer affirmed your sense of God's presence and your practice of prayer?*

_____

_____

_____

_____

_____

• *How has this reflection challenged your sense of God's presence and your understanding of prayer?*

_____

_____

_____

_____

_____

• *What do you need to do to expand your understanding, appreciation and practice of prayer?*

_____

_____

_____

_____

_____

Appendix 1

Prayers and Practices of the Catholic Community

Sign of the Cross

✝ In the name of the Father,
and of the Son,
and of the Holy Spirit. *Amen.*

Our Father

Our Father,
who art in heaven,
hallowed be your name;
your kingdom come;
your will be done
on earth as it is in heaven.
Give us this day our daily bread;
and forgive us our trespasses
as we forgive those who trespass against us;
and lead us not into temptation,
but deliver us from evil. *Amen.*

For yours is the kingdom,
and the power,
and the glory,
now and forever. *Amen.*

Glory Be to the Father

Glory be to the Father,
and to the Son,
and to the Holy Spirit.
As it was in the beginning,
is now, and will be forever. *Amen.*

Apostles' Creed

I believe in one God,
the Father Almighty,
   Creator of heaven and earth;
and in Jesus Christ,
   his only Son, our Lord,
   who was conceived by the Holy Spirit,
   born of the Virgin Mary,
   suffered under Pontius Pilate,
   was crucified, died, and was buried.
   He descended into hell;
   the third day he rose again from the dead.
   He ascended into heaven
   and sits at the right hand of God,
   the Father Almighty.
   From thence he shall come to judge
   the living and the dead.
I believe in the Holy Spirit,
   the holy catholic church,
   the communion of saints,
   the forgiveness of sins,
   the resurrection of the body
   and life everlasting. *Amen.*

The Beatitudes (Mt 5:3–10, Lk 6:20–25)

Blessed are the poor in spirit; the reign of God is theirs.

Blessed are the sorrowing; they shall be consoled.
Blessed are the lowly; they shall inherit the land.
Blessed are they who hunger and thirst for holiness; they shall have their fill.
Blessed are they who show mercy; mercy shall be theirs.
Blessed are the single-hearted; they shall see God.
Blessed are the peacemakers; they shall be called children of God.
Blessed are those persecuted for holiness' sake; the reign of God is theirs.

The Two Great Commandments (Mt 22:37–39)

You shall love the Lord your God with all your heart, with all your soul, and
    with all your mind.
You shall love your neighbor as yourself.

The Ten Commandments (Ex 20:1–21; Dt 5:1–22)

1. I am the Lord your God. . . . You shall not have strange gods before me.
2. You shall not take the name of the Lord your God in vain.
3. Remember to keep holy the Sabbath Day.
4. Honor your father and your mother.
5. You shall not kill.
6. You shall not commit adultery.
7. You shall not steal.
8. You shall not bear false witness against your neighbor.
9. You shall not covet your neighbor's wife.
10. You shall not covet your neighbor's goods.

Come, Holy Spirit

Come Holy Spirit,
fill the hearts of your faithful
and enkindle in them the fire of your love.

V. Send forth your Spirit and they shall be created.
R. And you shall renew the face of the earth.

Let us pray.
O God, who by the light of the Holy Spirit,
did instruct the hearts of your faithful,
grant that by that same Holy Spirit,

we may always be truly wise,
and ever rejoice in your consolation.
Through Christ our Lord. *Amen.*

The Jesus Prayer

Lord Jesus Christ,
Son of God,
have mercy on me a sinner.

The "O" Antiphons

O Wisdom, O holy Word of God
O Sacred Lord of ancient Israel
O Flower of Jesse's stem
O Key of David, O Royal Power of Israel
O Radiant dawn, splendor of eternal light, sun of justice
O King of all the nations
O Emmanuel, king and lawgiver

The Divine Praises

Blessed be God.
Blessed be his holy name.
Blessed be Jesus Christ, true God and true man.
Blessed be the name of Jesus.
Blessed be his most sacred heart.
Blessed be his most precious blood.
Blessed be Jesus in the most holy sacrament of the altar.
Blessed be the Holy Spirit, the paraclete.
Blessed be the great Mother of God, Mary most holy.
Blessed be her holy and immaculate conception.
Blessed be her glorious assumption.
Blessed be the name of Mary, virgin and mother.
Blessed be St. Joseph, her most chaste spouse.
Blessed be God in his angels and in his saints.

Act of Contrition

O my God,

I am heartily sorry for having offended you,
and I detest all my sins,
because of your just punishments,
but most of all because they offend you, my God,
who are all-good and deserving of all my love.
I firmly resolve, with the help of your grace,
to sin no more and to avoid the near occasion of sin.
Amen.

Act of Faith

O my God,
I firmly believe that you are one God
in three Divine Persons:
Father, Son, and Holy Spirit;
I believe that your Divine Son became man
and died for our sins,
and that he will come to judge the living and the dead.
I believe these and all the truths
which the holy catholic church teaches,
because you revealed them,
who can neither deceive nor be deceived.

Act of Hope

O my God,
relying on your infinite goodness and promises,
I hope to obtain pardon of my sins,
the help of your grace,
and life everlasting,
through the merits of Jesus Christ,
my Lord and Redeemer.

Act of Love

O my God,
I love you above all things,
with my whole heart and soul,
because you are all-good and worthy of all my love.

I love my neighbor as myself for the love of you.
I forgive all who have injured me,
and I ask pardon of all whom I have injured.

Stations of the Cross

We adore you O Christ and we bless you;
because by your holy cross
you have redeemed the world.

    I. Jesus is condemned to death.
    II. Jesus bears his cross.
    III. Jesus falls the first time.
    IV. Jesus meets his mother.
    V. Simon of Cyrene helps Jesus carry his cross.
    VI. Veronica wipes the face of Jesus.
    VII. Jesus falls a second time.
    VIII. Jesus meets the women of Jerusalem.
    IX. Jesus falls a third time.
    X. Jesus is stripped of his garments.
    XI. Jesus is nailed to the cross.
    XII. Jesus dies on the cross.
    XIII. Jesus is taken down from the cross.
    XIV. Jesus is placed in the tomb.

Hail Mary

Hail Mary, full of grace,
The Lord is with you!
blessed are you among women,
and blessed is the fruit of your womb, Jesus.
Holy Mary, Mother of God,
pray for us sinners,
now and at the hour of our death. *Amen.*

The Angelus

V. The angel of the Lord declared unto Mary.
R. And she conceived of the Holy Spirit.
   Hail Mary, . . .

V. "Behold the handmaid of the Lord.
R. Be it done unto me according to your word."
Hail Mary, . . .
V. And the Word was made flesh.
R. And dwelt among us.
Hail Mary, . . .
V. Pray for us, O holy Mother of God.
R. That we may be made worthy of the promises of Christ.

Let us pray:
Pour forth, we beseech you, O Lord,
your grace into our hearts,
that we to whom the incarnation of Christ, your Son,
was made known by the message of an angel,
may by his passion and cross
be brought to the glory of his resurrection,
through the same Christ our Lord. *Amen.*

Regina Caeli (Queen of Heaven)

Regina caeli, laetare, alleluia.
Quia quem meruisti portare, alleluia.
Resurrexit sicut dixit, alleluia.
Oro pro nobis Deum, alleluia.

Queen of heaven, rejoice, alleluia.
For he whom thou didst bear, alleluia.
Has risen as he said, alleluia.
Pray for us to God, alleluia.

Memorare

Remember, most gracious Virgin Mary,
never was it known
that anyone who fled to your protection,
implored your help,
or sought your intercession was left unaided.
Inspired by this confidence,
we fly unto you,
O Virgin of virgins, our mother.

To you we come;
before you we stand, sinful and sorrowful.
O Mother of the Word Incarnate,
despise not our petitions,
but in your clemency, hear and answer them. *Amen.*

Salve Regina (Hail Holy Queen)

Salve, Regina, mater misericordiae;
vita, dulcedo et spes nostra, salve.
Ad te clamamus, exsules filii Evae.
Ad te suspiramus, gementes et flentes
in hac lacrimarum valle.
Eia ergo, advocata nostra,
illis tuos misericordes oculos ad nos converte.
Et Jesus, benedictum fructum ventris tui,
nobis post hoc exsilium ostende.
O clemens, O pia, O dulcis Virgo Maria.

Hail, holy queen, Mother of mercy,
Hail, our life, our sweetness and our hope.
To you do we cry, the children of Eve.
To you do we send up our sighs,
mourning and weeping in this valley of tears.
Turn, then, most gracious advocate,
your eyes of mercy toward us;
and after this, our exile,
show unto us the blessed fruit of your womb, Jesus.
O clement, O loving, O sweet Virgin Mary. *Amen.*

The Mysteries of the Rosary

[Sign of the Cross, Apostle's Creed, Our Father, 3 Hail Marys, Glory Be, First
    Mystery, Our Father, 10 Hail Marys (decade), Glory Be, Second
    Mystery . . .]

Joyful Mysteries
1. The annunciation (Luke 1:38)
2. The visitation (Luke 1:39–40)
3. The nativity (Luke 2:7)

4. The presentation (Luke 2:39)
5. The finding of Jesus in the temple (Luke 2:46)

Sorrowful Mysteries
1. The agony in the garden (Matthew 26:39)
2. The scourging at the pillar (John 19:1)
3. The crowning with thorns (Mark 15:16–17)
4. The carrying of the cross (John 19:17)
5. The crucifixion (John 19:28–30)

Glorious Mysteries
1. The resurrection (Matthew 28:6)
2. The ascension (Matthew 28:20)
3. The descent of the Holy Spirit (Acts 4:31)
4. The assumption of Mary (Matthew 25:34)
5. The coronation of Mary (Revelation 12:1)

Grace before meals

Bless us, O Lord,
and these your gifts,
which we are about to receive
from your goodness,
through Christ, our Lord. *Amen.*

Thanksgiving after meals

We give you thanks
for all your benefits,
almighty God, who lives and reigns forever.
May the souls of the faithful departed,
through the mercy of God,
rest in peace. *Amen.*

Liturgical Seasons

Advent—four weeks before Christmas beginning on the Sunday which falls on
or closest to November 30.
Christmas season—Christmas until the Sunday after Epiphany or after January 6.

Lent—Ash Wednesday until Wednesday before Easter.
Paschal Triduum—Holy Thursday through evening prayer of Easter.
Easter season (Great 50 days)—Easter to Pentecost.
Ordinary Time—other 33–34 weeks of the year.

Corporal Works of Mercy

- To feed the hungry.
- To give drink to the thirsty.
- To clothe the naked.
- To visit the imprisoned.
- To shelter the homeless.
- To visit the sick.
- To bury the dead.

Spiritual Works of Mercy

- To admonish the sinner.
- To instruct the ignorant.
- To counsel the doubtful.
- To comfort the sorrowful.
- To bear wrongs patiently.
- To forgive all injuries.
- To pray for the living and the dead.

Seven Christian Virtues

- Theological virtues:
  faith
  hope
  charity
- Cardinal (moral) virtues:
  prudence
  justice
  temperance
  fortitude

Seven Capital Sins

- Pride

- Covetousness
- Lust
- Anger
- Gluttony
- Envy
- Sloth

Gifts of the Holy Spirit (Isaiah 11:2–3)

- Wisdom
- Understanding
- Counsel
- Fortitude
- Knowledge
- Piety
- Fear of the Lord

Fruits of the Spirit (Galatians 5:22–23)

- Charity
- Joy
- Peace
- Patience
- Kindness
- Goodness
- Long-suffering
- Humility
- Fidelity
- Modesty
- Continence
- Chastity

Holy Days of Obligation (U.S.A.)

Mary, Mother of God: January 1
Ascension Thursday: 40 days after Easter
Assumption of Mary: August 15
All Saints: November 1
Immaculate Conception: December 8

Christmas: December 25

Regulations concerning Fast and Abstinence

Fasting is refraining from eating three full meals during the day (usually, one full meal and two lighter meals). Days of fast apply to Catholics from the ages of 21 to 59, although those who are sick are not required to fast. In the United States, Ash Wednesday and Good Friday are days of fasting.

Abstinence is refraining from eating meat. This regulation applies to Catholics 14 years old and older. In the United States, Ash Wednesday, Good Friday and all Fridays of Lent are days of abstinence.

Precepts of the Church [i.e. duties expected of Catholic Christians]

1. To participate at mass on Sundays and holydays of obligation.
2. To fast and abstain on days appointed.
3. To receive the sacrament of penance at least once a year.
4. To receive the eucharist during Easter time.
5. To contribute to the support of the parish church and school.
6. To observe the marriage laws of the church.

Regulations regarding the Eucharistic Fast

Proper disposition is presumed in order to celebrate the eucharist. This includes: living in the state of grace (i.e., free from mortal sin), the right intention (to please God, not routine), and the observance of the eucharistic fast.

The eucharistic fast requires one to refrain from eating or drinking anything (other than water) one hour prior to reception of the eucharist. The sick and aged need fast for only 15 minutes. Furthermore, the sick may take nonalcoholic beverages and medications without any time limit.

Appendix 2

Sponsor Formation Sessions

Perhaps one of the most important ministries in initiation second only to the role of the local community—is the support and care given by sponsors and godparents. Catechumens and sponsors meet regularly to discuss the basic concerns, hopes, and fears that develop as the catechumen listens to God's call in his or her life.

Sponsorship is an important service, and therefore, the team needs to be cautious about who sponsors. Idealistically, everyone in the community is called to be a sponsor. However, given the limits that surround us, we want to provide the best possible experience for the catechumen as he or she journeys in faith with this community. A sponsor sensitive to the needs of the catechumen will be of great assistance in this journey.

Sponsors need to be informed up front that their ministry will involve a large commitment of time: regular gatherings with the catechumen, witnessing for the community, and catechetical sessions.

The ministry of sponsor has two important aspects: the commitment of the sponsors to fulfill the responsibilities entrusted to them, and the commitment of the parish to provide all the necessary resources and support the sponsors need in order to fulfill those responsibilities. One way a parish responds to this need is to provide regular gatherings for sponsors.

The formation of sponsors (and godparents, whenever possible) is similar to the formation of the initiation team, with stronger emphasis on faith-sharing skills, shared prayer, reflection on the scriptures, discernment, conversion theories, and communication skills. Sponsors need to be sensitive to the fact that choosing to affiliate with a community is both a joyful and a painful process. There is a death to an old way of life, and the catechumen will often experience something akin to grieving.

Regular gatherings for sponsors will help them talk about what's going on, as well as keep them informed of any developments. Sponsor coordinators, when providing sponsor formation gatherings, can use this handbook as a sourcebook. The handbook was developed, in fact, for primary use in small group gatherings of sponsors, facilitated by someone familiar with the material.

The social sciences and learning theorists support both the value and importance of adults working in small groups. In such cooperative learning environments, adults are able to explore together various dimensions of an issue, learning from the insights of their peers.

When using this handbook for sponsor formation gatherings, the sponsor coordinator will want to supplement and expand some of the material contained in the handbook. The following suggestions are meant to assist the sponsor coordinator in this task.

Chapter 1: Christian Initiation

Chapter 1 is intended to provide a basic foundation and introduction to the Order of Christian Initiation of Adults. Many sponsors will come with a pre-conciliar view of sacrament, or with the perception that initiation is another parish program. The sponsor coordinator will want to develop Chapter 1 with:

> • *Basic introduction to an understanding of sacraments since Vatican Council II.*
> • *Reinforcement of the Order of Christian Initiation of Adults as ritual sacrament, not a program.*
> • *Introduction to the language of the Order and the distinction between the various periods and stages.*
> • *Clarification regarding the distinctions in the status and celebration of the unbaptized and baptized (uncatechized and catechized).*
> • *Importance of understanding the Order within the contexts of the liturgical calendar.*

Chapter 2: Conversion: Falling in Love

Chapter 2 looks at the heart of Christian initiation—conversion. Many sponsors will equate conversion with highly-charged affective experiences, and therefore will doubt that they have had any conversion experiences. In order to help the sponsor make the shift from program to sacrament, they will need to spend time reflecting on conversion and its place in their own lives. The sponsor coordinator will want to develop Chapter 2 with:

• *Critical reflection on the meaning and experience of conversion.*
• *Exploration of the multiple dimensions of conversion, such as moral, affective, and theistic.*
• *The specific relationship of sponsors to someone in the experience of conversion in initiation.*
• *The need to continually reflect and pray about personal experiences of conversion.*

Chapter 3: The Ministry of Sponsor

Chapter 3 explores the specifics of the ministry of sponsoring, placing special focus on expectations rather than a step-by-step exploration of responsibilities, which will be discussed in Chapter 4. This chapter sets out the foundations of sponsoring. The sponsor coordinator will want to develop Chapter 3 with:

• *Importance of sacramental sponsorship.*
• *Importance of the community as sponsor and the community's role in providing the foundation for personal sponsorship.*
• *Vision of the ministry of the baptized that leads to differentiation of ministries rather than distinctions.*
• *Highlighting how the order of the faithful live discipleship.*
• *Particular expectations of sponsors in your parish.*

Chapter 4: Celebrating Initiation: The Role of Sponsors

Chapter 4 expands the introduction to the Order of Christian Initiation of Adults given in Chapter 1, and is intended to be returned to throughout the initiation process. Prior to the beginning of a particular period or stage, the sponsors need to review in greater detail their responsibilities. The sponsor coordinator will want to develop Chapter 4 with:

- *Specific information about the particular period or stage in your parish community.*
- *The role and importance of discernment for the celebration of the rites.*
- *Ritual preparation with the sponsors for each celebration.*
- *The purpose and manner of giving testimony.*
- *Familiarity with ability of symbols to unleash power and help appropriate meaning by their encounter, especially with regard to the Easter Vigil.*
- *Sponsor coordinator will want to consult a concordance for scripture references for symbols of the Easter Vigil.*

Chapter 5: Presence: Being Truly Present to Another

Chapter 5 focuses on developing communication skills. Since there is a lot of material in this chapter—both information and exercises—the sponsor coordinator might choose to develop this section over two sessions. Also, the sponsor coordinator needs to be intentional about these skills in all the sponsor workshops so that sponsors learn through imitation as well as presentation. The sponsor coordinator will want to develop Chapter 5 with:

- *Distinction between casual and intentional use of skills.*
- *Difference between hearing and active listening.*
- *Modifying and expanding exercises for particular group.*
- *Keep sponsors focused but not preoccupied on developing the skills so that the catechumen remains primary focus (not the skills).*
- *Helping sponsors articulate feelings in constructive ways.*
- *Exploring the process of transforming assumptions.*

Chapter 6: Growth: Helping Another to Grow

Chapter 6 looks at the development of trust in relationships. Using an artificial chart of the development of relationships, the chapter helps highlight the place of the sponsoring relationship within the larger schema of relationships. The sponsor coordinator will want to develop Chapter 6 with:

• *Helping sponsors struggle with relational issues—sponsoring is not the time for instant intimacy or professional distance.*
• *Distinguishing terms (and affirming the appropriateness of the distinctions): acquaintance, colleague, companion, friend, significant other, and the like.*
• *Helping sponsor articulate reasonable boundaries for the sponsoring relationship, including questions of time and availability.*
• *Exploring the notion of co-dependency and how to avoid dysfunctional qualities in the sponsoring relationship.*

Chapter 7: Self-Disclosure: Affirming the Story of Oneself and Another

Chapter 7 explores the processes of storytelling and questioning, affirming the value of both in the spiritual journey. The sponsor coordinator will want to develop Chapter 7 with:

• *Varieties of storytelling styles.*
• *Finding God in the ordinary of life, spirituality of the marketplace.*
• *Universal call to holiness.*
• *Work on distinguishing between stories and history (and how truth is found in both in different ways).*
• *Value of helping self and others ask better questions, not necessarily to find answers.*

Chapter 8: Mystery: Fostering a Heightened Sense of Mystery

Chapter 8 places the rest of the handbook within the context of the developing relationship with God. It attempts to remind sponsors that all the skills, however helpful, gain their importance within this context: helping others (and self) embrace the demands of the mission of the reign of God. The sponsor coordinator will want to develop Chapter 8 with:

- *Discussion on the importance and development of God-images.*
- *Varieties of prayer styles in the traditions (apophatic, kataphatic, etc.)*
- *Essential link between personal prayer and communal worship.*
- *Celebration of the rites of the Order of Christian Initiation of Adults as prayer.*

What do I need in my life now to be more faithful to God's call